UNDERSTANDING THE CONNECTION BETWEEN BLACK AND ABORIGINAL PEOPLES

The Links Between African-American, Black, Native American and Indigenous Cultures

By Raging BlakkIndian Dub

ISBN: 0-973091 l-4-2 (Paperback)

TFTT –The Fire This Time Pub. Toronto, San Francisco

Canadian edition published by The Fire This Time: Toronto, Canada
Library of Congress control number 2002105711
National Library of Canada Cataloguing in Publication Data.
Dub, Raging BlakkIndian.

Understanding the Connection between Black and Aboriginal Peoples
ISBN 0-9730911-4-2. 1. Indigenous peoples –America. 2. Africans Americans Relations with Indians. I Title. E98.R28D82 2002 303.48'2C2002-910471- 8onto.
Also available multimedia CD Rom "The Black Indian Connection: music, video, politics" ISBN 0-9730911-2-6 which contains complete book text, photos plus 22 min BlakkIndian documentary, 'Dancing on John Wayne's Head' and film 'In the Beginning' winner of Reel World Film Festival (Toronto, Canada) award for best short film.
This CD Rom available from: tftt3000@yahoo.ca.
audio book also available from: tftt3000@yahoo.ca.

Introduction

This book is a result of a long trek throughout the world lasting thirteen years seeking to thread together academic research with oral testimonies and histories obtained on location in over thirty countries. The aim is to provide the reader with a new contemporary look at the Blakk Indian connection encompassing music, arts, resistance and politics always guided by the ancient historical ties that have existed between Black and Native American and various Indigenous cultures.

Throughout this book I use the term "Blakk Indian" this is a term that I have coined to describe the mixture between Black, African, African-American peoples with Native American, Indigenous and Aboriginal peoples and cultures. (Obviously we still struggle to find descriptive words for these respective races and cultures that are clearly understood and accepted by all) To discuss this and other issues please feel free to contact the author via email at: tftt3000@yahoo.ca.

Credits

Sections of the book was edited by Melville Dessalines Slyver

Proofread by Jahteecha

Front cover and graphic design: Dubdem

Front cover photo by Michael P. Smith © 1992

All photographs by mapuchedub c. copyright 2000 except for Photographs for New Orleans Chapter which were taken by Michael P. Smith c. copyright 1992

Sonic dub bass frequencies: Bobby Marshall and Asian Dub Foundation

Photo of Marcelo "troublemaker" Yuka from Brasil by Felipe Varanda

Additional colour photos accompanying this book can be viewed at

http://www.firethistime.com

TABLE OF CONTENTS

Supai Reservation

Supai Reservation

For a second, I couldn't believe my eyes. I had just passed the slogan "Roots, Rock, Reggae" spray-painted on a huge boulder, yet I wasn't in Jamaica or any of the better-known reggae strongholds. I was in the Grand Canyon about to enter the most isolated aboriginal reservation in the United States. After a long journey I realized that I was suddenly very close to meeting what has been described as one of the most intriguing set of reggae fans in the world: the Havasupai Indians.

Flipping through the pages of a Reggae Beat magazine, I had come across an article reporting on the first reggae concert held on the Supai reservation. The reaction of the residents, the Havasupai, to reggae was depicted in such overwhelmingly enthusiastic terms that I wanted to find out more than what was in this brief article and to see for myself if these reggae fans were indeed a reality.

A few months later I arrived in Phoenix, Arizona and then took a bus to Kingman. I was immediately provided with an insight into the racial climate of Arizona (a state which at one time fought against having a day to honor Martin Luther King's birthday). Shortly after my bus pulled into the town an elderly aboriginal man stopped me at the door of the bus station and asked me for some money for food. As I gave him some change a burly white man charged out of a Salvation Army office and started screaming at me for giving the old man money. I told him to chill out and continued on my way.

As I stepped on the famous Route 66 highway, white state troopers pulled up, roughly threw me up against a wall and told me in no uncertain terms that I wasn't welcome there.

I managed to get to a shopping center where I was told Hualapi Indians came to shop and therefore existed the chance of a ride.

After several hours without seeing any possibilities of a lift, I was very surprised to see the same old man I had given money to, appear on the scene. He offered to find a ride for me. Sure enough fifteen minutes later the two of us were riding in the back of an open pick up truck. After fifty-five miles of traveling through a torrential rainstorm while being pelted by hailstones the size of golf balls, we both got off at Hualapi reservation located at Peach Springs.

It was a very tiny reserve containing a restaurant, a gas station and general store. The man who had gotten me the ride told me I could spend the night at his house, a small bare wooden shack on the reserve.

In an attempt to dry off I went for a walk. After a while I thought I heard the sounds of the reggae group Black Uhuru, somewhere in the distance, but I couldn't be certain. As I turned the corner, I realized their distinctive sound was indeed booming in front of the general store. A scene reminiscence of what I had often witnessed in Jamaica was happening. A group of Hualapi Indian youth garbed in a colourful variety of reggae paraphernalia were skanking with wild abandon to the reggae music.

As I came closer someone spotted me and the group all turned around to check out the person with dreadlocked hair coming towards them. At first they were cool and aloof. But after someone asked me where I was from, the ice broke and I was literally mobbed by people who wanted to touch my dreadlocks and welcome me there.

The next morning my host arranged for me to be taken to a point where all cars going to Supai would have to pass. When I was dropped off, I found myself in the middle of a vast arid but breathtaking Arizona landscape complete with blowing tumbleweeds. I waited for the greater part of a day here and just as I was getting worried about being stranded, a car pulled up and gave me a ride to the Hualapi hilltop, which was the entry point to the Havasupai reservation.

The hilltop was completely deserted and the only thing I could hear was the sound of the wind blowing fiercely. In front of me was a spectacular view of the Grand Canyon with all of its copper coloured rock formations. As I looked around I noticed some of the ochre coloured boulders on the hilltop had Bob Marley song titles spray painted on them!!

The serenity of the mountaintop was broken by the sound of the movements of a mule.

Sitting astride the mule was a Havasupai youth wearing a red headband, a Bob Marley T-shirt, red, gold, and green armbands and a variety of reggae buttons pinned to his jean jacket. He greeted me with the words "Irie" a common greeting in Jamaica. He offered to take me on the fourteen-mile journey to the bottom of the Grand Canyon where Supai was located.

I climbed on the mule behind him and popped a cassette of reggae dub music into the portable tape player he was carrying. The heavy drum and bass sounded stupendous as it bounced off the walls of the Grand Canyon. Every other second it seemed like the mule was about to plunge off the very narrow and precipitous trail. However it quickly became apparent that the mule was well acquainted with the twists and turns of the trail, so I decided to just enjoy the beautiful scenery and the accompanying dub soundtrack.

After a few hours of riding we arrived at the bottom of the Grand Canyon and entered Supai. It's lush green fields and small houses lined up along the pathways reminded me of rural Jamaica. The sound of a waterfall could be heard in the distance and people were hanging about or traveling around on horseback. As I made my way through the village practically every house I passed had some kind of reggae music coming from it and several Havasupai walked around with boom boxes that were blasting reggae.

Supai was so isolated that some food supplies had to be flown in by government helicopters. When I entered the community general store I was really struck by how much of the supplies brought in was junk food! Later on a nurse in the community told me that obesity and diabetes had become a major health problem with aboriginal people in the region. This problem had become prevalent when the government started shipping in cheaply priced junk food, which had displaced the traditional diet. I was reminded of a parallel example in Canada where on some reservations government subsides had made it cheaper to buy alcohol than to purchase milk!

The Havasupai really made me feel welcome and I spent a lot of time conversing with a Havasupai reggae fan called Benjamin. Like most of the Havasupai that I met, Benjamin had listened to so much reggae from Jamaica that he spoke Jamaican patois. Another common practice in Supai was people to quote reggae lyrics in order to make a point! Benjamin as a result of listening to reggae had become a Rastafarian.

He explained how the Havasupai loved the Rastafarian colours red, gold and green because for them red stood for the people; the earth and the red canyon walls; green represented the trees; and gold the sun. Benjamin told me that Bob Marley had been the first reggae artist to be heard in Supai. One story told was that some aboriginal people from California were listening to Bob Marley's Positive Vibrations album on the Havasupai hilltop and gave a copy to a Havasupai who took it down to Supai. Supai's residents made copies and it spread like wildfire! It was easy to tell that Bob Marley was the most popular reggae artist in Supai and his impact on the Havasupai is something that cannot be underestimatd. One of the most amazing pieces of information that I learnt first hand by being in Supai was that Havasupai prophesies state that legendary resistance fighter Chief Crazy Horse would return in the form of a black man. The Havasupai believe that Bob Marley is the fulfillment of this prophesy!! As the Havasupai battle against destructive uranium mining on their territory, Bob Marley's lyrics are often quoted as inspiration for their anti-mining struggle. For example on several occasions I heard people saying, "none but ourselves can free our minds" which is a verse from Marley's Redemption Song.

The affinity the Havasupai have for Marley's song was perfectly illustrated by the following account that was told to me by Havasupai activist.

"Bob Marley has been a very inspirational figure to the Havasuapi, to the young people to the little people to the older people. I walked into a room once where there was an eighty year old listening to Bob Marley singing and she was in tears. The music was Redemption Song. I said, "What's the matter?" and she said, "I like the words here. It reminds me of the prayers of the old people -the way they used to pray. It reaches down into the soul -the spiritual soul -way down in there." I said to her "I'm glad you are crying because I feel the same way every time I hear it."

Many Havasupai relate to reggae lyrics because of the similarity of oppression faced by black and aboriginal people. One Havasupai reggae fan informed me "we feel really close with the music of reggae because we are struggling and striving as much as the black people who have been afflicted by the governments that have taken over their homelands. I feel that the same afflictions and prejudice that has happened to black people have happened to the American Indian people. Reggae music brings our people, the black and American Indian people together." Misuse of the land is a common concern among the Havasuapi and reggae lyrics.

Jamaican dub poet Mutaburuaka has stated black and aboriginal people have similar problems and this "is because of the land which was taken away from both sets of people. You'll find the lyrics necessarily catch on because the sentiment there is the same. The quest for control, for ownership of the land, the quest to be free in your own place, to be able to control your own destiny and environment."

On his album, The Mystery Unfolds, Mutaburuaka notes in America, "The true owners of your nation are forced to live on a reservation." When Jamaican artists Michigan and Smiley performed on the nearby Hopi reservation the audience responded enthusiastically when they changed the words of their song "black awareness" and instead sang:

There was a time in Indian history /
there was no slavery or brutality /
No sadness and no misery /
no confusion no sick mentality /
the time has come for every Indian to know himself /
And fight against downpression /
We call it Indian awareness.

Freddie McGregor also played at that gig which was held on June 6, 1984. It was the first reggae concert to be held on a Hopi reserve. In an interview with Hein Marais he remarked "The first feeling I got was that they were very similar to Jamaicans in their mood and vibes. What I have learnt is that they share the same struggle that we are going through and that's what makes them very close to us"

Traditional Singer and Reggae fan Andy

Kingston, Jamaica

Kingston, Jamaica

While I was in Supai one of the things that really caught my attention was the large number of Havasupai who had a deep appreciation for the experimental dub music of Rastafarian, Augustus Pablo. Most of the Havasupai I spoke with told me what drew them to his music was "the very spiritual vibe" they felt that was coming from his music.

When I arrived in Jamaica one of the first things I did was to contact Augustus Pablo. The legendary musician is known as a very reclusive figure. I had first become acquainted with him when we collaborated on a project in support of indigenous rights. Knowing Augustus as deeply spiritual person who was very supportive of the struggles of aboriginal peoples I was eager to tell him about my experience in Supai.

Later, I met up with Augustus at his home where he was reasoning (Jamaican slang meaning to philosophize and to discuss), with another Rastafarian elder Cudjoe. Augustus was very happy to hear that the Havasupai had tapped into the spiritual feeling of his compositions since that was the key to his music. As we were discussing the Havasupai the elder told me a story that put Bob Marley's relationship with aboriginal people in a new light. Very few people know that Bob Marley arranged for one of the great grandsons of the famed aboriginal resistance leader Chief Joesph to come to Jamaica to reason with Rastafarian elders. Chief Joesph's great grandsons stayed at Cudjoe's house.

Cudjoe recounted how one night his guest woke up and stated he was unable to sleep and that he had felt the spirits of his ancestors who were crying out for a proper burial. I decided to do some research on the existence of (aboriginal peoples from Turtle Island an aboriginal term for the continent of North America) being present in Jamaica. What I discovered looking through archival documents was the fact aboriginal people from Turtle Island had actually been sold into slavery in Jamaica! In particular after the Pequot English war in New England, many aboriginal prisoners were enslaved and sold in the West Indies. From 1670 onwards the British in South Carolina regularly engaged in the slave trade, sending tens of thousands of aboriginal people to the West Indies and other markets. It had been documented that in 1674 a group of Cherokees was sent to Jamaica and in 1693 a Cherokee delegation at Charleston unsuccessfully requested the return of their relatives who had been taken to Jamaica.

Cudjoe's account had led me to information about the presence of aboriginal people from Turtle Island, which was simply unavailable to the general public especially since most information on slavery is focused on the African slave trade.

While I was in Jamaica I had a conversation with a Blakk Indian artist Colin F. who was of African and Carib Indian ancestry. One of the topics we discussed was the total lack of reference to the original inhabitants of Jamaica, the Arawak Indians. Typically in Jamaican schools the only reference made to the Arawarks is they existed in Jamaica till the arrival of the Spanish colonialists who wiped them out. Afterwards African slaves were brought in to replace the exterminated Arawaks, is the history taught in schools. The implication being that Africans and Arawaks had no contact with one another. Yet I spoke with some archaeologists working with a historical institute in Jamaica who had made what they described as a landmark discovery, which contradicted this theory. These archaeologists had found a Maroon (run away African Slaves) village way in the hills of central Jamaica. In this village they had found Arawak pottery but they also used the term 'syncretic' to describe the pottery, meaning it was a synthesis of two cultures; Arawak and Maroon. The pottery they found indicated that the Arawaks and the Maroons had lived together and influenced each other to the degree that they had created a new form of pottery. They also found in a cave three Arawaks spiritual masks and one of these masks had African features on it. Evidently there was a greater degree of intermarriage and cultural exchange that we had ever been led to believe. One of the probabilities of this points to is that there is also a number of Jamaicans who have both African and Arawak Indian blood.

To understand the significance of the original aboriginal inhabitants of Jamaica I spoke to Afua Cooper a Jamaican dub poet, and historian.

In 1985 on the cassette, Poetry Is Not Luxury, Afua Cooper in her piece "Christopher Columbus" for the first time in recorded Jamaican music described in great detail the genocide inflicted on the aboriginal inhabitants in the Caribbean.

Afua felt it made sense that some Arawaks had escaped into the mountains and had shown fugitive African slaves the way to elude the Spanish and to survive on the island. It was Afua's contention that in the Eastern Caribbean there was a greater awareness of the Carib presence. She had met a lot of artists from the Eastern Caribbean such as dub poet Ras Mo, who were of both African and Carib ancestry and who publicly acknowledged this. Trinidadian musician Brother Resistance is known for one of his compositions, which is highly critical of Christopher Columbus. When I spoke with him he told me it's important that people become aware of the Holocaust that happened to Native people" unfortunately at this moment the media image of John Wayne and cowboys and Indian movies is what dominates people's imagination. He felt that it is very significant that when Africans got their freedom on Hispaniola, they renamed it Haiti, which is an Arawak name. They didn't call their new republic "Little Africa" or "New Congo" they called it Haiti in recognition of the first owners of the land.

Afua Cooper in the foreword to her poetry book "Memories Have Tongues" wrote that she believed the mythologies of the Arawaks "went underground and later resurface in the words of the present people inhabiting the island". One of her poems is about the Arawak goddess Atabeyra. Referring to this Afua told me that: "I don't think I can speak of the history of the Caribbean without making reference to the original inhabitants, who in the case of Jamaica were Arawak people. For me, as an individual who has, a deep sense of history and place, acknowledging and recognizing these people who were in these places before the African presence is vital. Black peoples history did not begin with slavery, but slavery was such a crucial point in our history that we keep referring back to it. At the same time the history of Jamaica didn't begin with Black and European people coming into the island there was a history prior to that."

Jamaican dub poet Binta Breeze of Arawak Indian ancestry, very eloquently provides us with some lessons and insights into the position of aboriginal people as caretakers of the land and how that position has been disrespected over the course of history. "On any land that makes up this planet called Earth, there were people that were put there by the Creator and who by the very fact that they were the first people of the land share an understanding of that land, how to tread on that land, how to live on that land without destroying it. How to love that land as something given to one to take care of. So I think that whoever we are, where ever we come from, when we are on somebody's land, we want to make contact in an extremely humble way with the Native people that the Creator has blessed with the knowledge of that land. Part of our problem is that often when we go onto other people's land we walk with such arrogance. Sometimes we bring with us a mentality that says because we have certain things we have more power and we misinterpret the humility of the people who know and love that land".

Wilson Harris a Black writer from Guyana makes constant references to aboriginal cultures like the Mayan, Aztecs and Arawaks. Guyana was the site of revolt in 1687 where African and Arawak Indians revolted against occupying colonialists. His book "Palace of the Peacocks" set in Guyana has Blakk Indian characters.

He is another key figure who in his writing has sought to give recognition to the original aboriginal inhabitants of the Caribbean and South America and their subsequent impact on the region. In "Hougan and Shaman" he writes:

"Now one knows that the New World has written into it many unlawful and alien elements. The very ground beneath us had been stolen. I think that's why Proudhon wrote his book Property Is Theft. Wherever one looks, we know the land was stolen either from the American Indian, who were decimated and thrust off this land, or stolen from Mexico or whatever. So there are unlawful elements written into our society at the base of our civilization."

Jamaican dub poet Oku Onuora takes this point a step forward with his contribution to the Blakk Indian recording project, Dancing on John Wayne's Head.

In his poem "Ohtokin" Oku in recognition of the continued injustice faced by aboriginal people emphatically states, "that there can be no justice on stolen land!"

Throughout the Caribbean there exists an educational system which is still propagating a colonialist view of history that negates the presence and contribution of both African and aboriginal people.

Radical people in this region fighting to counteract this have focused most of their energy in reclaiming the African side of their heritage. The lack of knowledge about their aboriginal heritage has affected people's perception of themselves in countries like Jamaica where people will tend to think of their identity in terms of only their African ancestry instead of looking at the real possibility that they have a Blakk Indian heritage.

Until there are more writers and educators like Wilson Harris and Afua Cooper making Caribbean people more conscious of their aboriginal roots it will always be difficult to accurately assess Blakk Indian history and identity in the Caribbean.

Augustus Pablo

Costa Rica

Costa Rica

One of the most dynamic case studies in the history of Black and Aboriginal interaction that I have personally uncovered takes place in the village of Puerto Veijo, located on the Caribbean coast of Costa Rica. Not only had I not heard or read anything about the history of this region in North America but I found that within the country of Costa Rica itself, specific information on this syncretic culture was very scant. No one has seen fit to do a specific investigation of this particular history.

Puerto Veijo is situated near the border of Panama. With the recent opening of roads into the region, the village has become a popular tourist resort for surfers. I was directed to this area as one of the few places in Costa Rica where one could find a concentrated Black population. In fact renown Jamaican political visionary Marcus Garvey traveled there doing political organizing with Black people who came from the Caribbean to work on the construction of the Panama Canal.

As I traveled on the dusty road to Puerto Veijo, I realized that I wasn't in a region that just had Black people. This realization came to me as I examined the faces of the people getting on the bus I was riding. The majority of passengers had facial features that were like Blakk Indians I had seen in other countries. (i.e. thick lips and thin slanted eyelids)

Upon my arrival at the sleepy seaside village of Puerto Veijo I went in search of some food. I ended up in the small home style restaurant owned by an elderly woman in her sixties who was affectionately called "Miss Sam". After savoring her Jamaican style cooking I inquired about her family history. Like others I had seen on the bus, she had features which suggested both Black and Aboriginal ancestry.

"Miss Sam" explained to me how her mother was a Mosquito Indian from Nicaragua and her father was from Jamaica. In response to my statement that most of the people I had seen appeared to have Blakk Indian ancestry she replied that I was correct; and that the main families in Puerto Veijo were descendants of Bribri Indians and Black people who intermarried. She directed me to the home of Maurico, a Bribri Indian who lived in the mountains, someone whom she indicated was extremely knowledgeable about the Blakk Indian history of this area.

The next day I made the trek to Maurico's home in the nearby mountains. Everywhere was especially green following fresh rains. I could see monkeys and colourful parrots in the canopies of the trees. I was greeted by a very easy going man who at the moment was spending time with his children and listening to Bob Marley tapes. He lived in a traditional Bribri house which was a tall wooden structure with a thatched roof made of coconut leaves. Maurico divided his time working as a guide for tourists in the jungle and working with the local ecological association to protect the beaches and rainforests.

I asked him to provide me with a history of the region. According to Maurico the Bribri Indians had inhabited this area. Then over two hundred years ago some Black maroons had journeyed here from Columbia and Nicaragua. Since the beaches of Puerto Veijo were rich in turtles, these voyagers would stop and look for meat and turtle shells and leave when they had sufficient cargo.

Impressed with the beauty of the land the maroons returned and began planting the food they used at home i.e. yam, cassava, oranges and different types of roots.

When they came back the following year and saw these crops were producing; some decided to bring their families from Columbia to live on the coast of Puerto Veijo.

At this time the Bribri were having problems with raiding by Aboriginal people from Nicaragua. As a safeguard the Bribri left the beaches and moved inland. Maurico recounts at first the Bribri were shy about these new people, wondering if perhaps they were their adversaries from Nicaragua. After observing them for a period of time the Bribri concluded that these weren't their foes and went down to the beach to meet them.

The Bribri would spend nights with the maroons and together the two peoples would hunt and collect turtle shells. Maurico told me "The black people were regarded simply as friends and there never was war between them". It is worth noting that during this time period the Bribri put up such a fierce resistance to encroaching Spanish colonists, that the Spaniards were unable to penetrate this region of Costa Rica. As more Black people moved to Puerto Veijo the Bribri would go to the beach to trade with items like salt which came from the inland. From the maroons the Bribri would gain knowledge about what was happening in the outside world especially about the expansion activities of the Spanish and other European colonialists. In turn the Bribri passed on information about life in the mountains. As a result of this growing contact Black people went inland with some marrying Bribri and remaining there. Maurico told me that right now one could go into the mountains and find Indian families with kinky hair and dark skin, as he put it "the friendship between these two people produced some new flowers and this is much of the people you find right now".

The Bribri did what they could to help Black people survive in the region. They taught the maroons about the fruits and roots they used and how to make fermented drinks from local plants.

The Bribri instructed them how to take care of snakebites and other poisons in the area. In return the Black people demonstrated ways of using plants and fruits in ways that they had never thought of. Previously the Bribri had only used the coconut occasionally as fruit while the Black people showed them how to use it as a base for cooking, i.e., making rice and beans with coconut. A similar process occurred with the use of cassava. Traditionally the Bribri would only take the cassava and roast it; Black people taught them how to make flour from it. The exchange of knowledge was such that now Maurico says, "when we look for roots we don't know where it comes from – whether its from the Blacks or from the Indians, often you get confused because we both use the same plant."

Maurcio himself when growing up would spend half the year living on the more Caribbean influenced coast with Black people. He confided in me that he used to be a huge soul music fan and used to sport an Afro. The other half of the year he would live in mountains in a traditional Bribri household. His life reflected a pattern of friendship and interaction that was common in this area and which had produced an atmosphere of trust between the two peoples. Later on I was provided with a striking example of this. I was walking really late at night on the dirt road leading back to Puerto Veijo. The only light was from a partially clouded over moon and my flashlight. Suddenly I heard a noise on the other side of the road coming from behind me. I realized I was visible from the moonlight and with my flashlight I could make out a small figure making their way to my side.

This in itself took me by surprise. The stereotyped association of Black people as being dangerous and violent is very prevalent in Costa Rica. So often during the course of my travels in Costa Rica I would notice people flinching and moving out of the way –often crossing over to the other side of the street when they saw my darker skin and dreadlocks. I had read an article in a Costa Rican newspaper that indicated that car rental companies would charge tourists a higher insurance rate when their destination is Puerto Veijo because of the expectation since there are more Black people living there this meant an increased possibility of crime.

My own flashlight revealed the small, hunched figure of a wizen Bribri man who looked to be in his fifties. A crocus bag full of coconuts was perched on his shoulders. He looked at me and gave me a warm toothless smile and just started walking by my side like it was the most natural thing in the world to do. Words seemed not only inappropriate but also completely unnecessary, as the two of us walked for the next hour on the deserted road. When we reached Puerto Veijo we shook hands and he continued on his way.

I was deeply touched by the degree of trust the old man had shown me and I immediately realized how communication and trust could exist between strangers who don't speak the same language. Often when people refer to the "natural" and inevitable hostility between groups who are different I like to recall my conversations and experiences in Puerto Veijo along with the following quote from Bell Hooks:

"Contrary to colonial white imperialistic insistence that it was "natural" for groups who are different to engage in conflict and power struggle, the first meeting of African and Native Americans offers a counter perspective, a vision of cross cultural contact where reciprocity and recognition of the primacy of community are affirmed, where the will to conquer and dominate was not seen as the only way to confront the other who is not ourselves."

Blakk Indian Children Puerto Veijo

Panama

Panama

My conversations with Maurico raised a lot of questions for me about Blakk Indians in this part of Central America. I started speculating about the existence of a possible pattern of Black Indian communities existing along Central America's Caribbean coast.

I was aware of the approximately 80,000 Garifuna who live along the northeast coast of this region with 12,000 being concentrated in the country of Belize.

The Garifuna are a product of Maroon African slaves intermarried with Carib Indians from St Vincent. They are known for retaining their own particular blend of syncretic culture, which contains a strong mixture of African and Carib Indian elements. Garifuna history in Belize began when a British vessel carrying Carib Indians from St Vincent who had been involved in a failed rebellion against the British was shipwrecked off the coast of Belize.

I had been told about the island of Livingstone not only known as a Garifuna stronghold on Guatemala's Caribbean coast but also for its Rastafarian population. My own research had informed me that Guatemala's first president Carrera was the son of an Aboriginal father and Black mother. Rallying oppressed black and Indian people around him, he overthrew the government and was named president for life. In 1627 a European traveler Thomas Gage reported the presence of three hundred Black runaways in the eastern region of Guatemala.

Nicaragua also had Black Indian communities on its Caribbean coast. All this fit into what I saw as a pattern of escaped African slaves (maroons) often establishing communities of resistance along the coast. After their interaction with the local aboriginal people Blakk Indian communities were formed. A black Indian independent state was established in 1599 near Esmeralda in Ecuador. Other Blakk Indian republics were established along the Caribbean coast and one called "Zamba de Nirgua" survived from the 16 th to the 19 th century.

The other contributing element to this equation was the existence of Black pirates or buccaneers. Off the coast of the Dominican Republic was the island of Tortuga, the chief buccaneer settlement in the Caribbean and Central America. The pirates who were chiefly English or French with some Spaniards and Dutch were always on the lookout for those with exceptional courage and fighting ability. They were quite willing to recruit runaway African slaves. Among escaped Africans were those from the Ashantis, Dahomey and Coramantee peoples who were know for their warrior abilities. Consequently these Africans were welcomed by the pirates with the result that a considerable proportion of pirates were Black. Some of the best pirate captains such as Roc Brasiliano and Diaguillo, who were proteges of sir Francis Drake, were Black. Bartholomews Roberts reputed to be one of the greatest pirates was described by Captain Charles Johnson, another pirate, as a "tall Black man nearly forty years of age".

These Black pirates also sailed along Central America's Caribbean coast establishing bases where they could hide out. While I didn't have the names of specific communities to go to, I was certain that if I made my way along the Caribbean coast that with a bit of luck I would find such a community which might also have a Blakk Indian population.

I decided to make my way to the islands of Boca Del Toro that were situated off the coast of Panama, a couple hours from Costa Rica. I had heard villagers in Puerto Veijo saying that they would sometimes take their boats there to go fishing and dive for lobsters. It was my thinking that it was possible that others in the distant past might have also done so. After a three-hour bus ride from Puerto Veijo to the Panamanian port of Almirante, I took a boat from there to Boca Del Toro. One had to pass through a myriad of small islands, many of which had the thatched huts of Guaymi Indians scattered along the shoreline. I disembarked at the main island of Boca Del Toro which had a small main street lined with a few stores and restaurants. After finding a room in a small hotel I started conversing with the teenage son of the proprietors' who were of Guaymi Indian decent. When I explained to him the information that I was seeking he directed me to one of the adjoining islands where this very knowledgeable elder named Beni lived.

The next day I took a canoe across the water to the nearby island. The crystal blue waters were filled with other boats with people diving for lobsters. These waters were known for their abundant marine life. As our boat made its way around the island to reach the docking area it was possible to see the thick wild vegetation that covered most of the island. The island seemed to be filled with the faces of people with Blakk Indian features except this time there was an additional twist.

Everyone spoke a dialect that not only had English, Spanish and Guaymi but also distinctively evident was Jamaican patois and a thick Jamaican accent.

When I asked for Beni, one of the parents directed their child to take me to his house. After some walking, we stopped at a small tiled house that was perched on the side of a hill overlooking the bay. I asked if Beni was home. A couple of minutes later a very old man appeared accompanied by a young child whom it turned out was his granddaughter who assisted him into a chair.

I expressed to Beni my desire to understand the history of the island. The first thing Beni said to me was that outsiders never got the history of the island correct. It was unbelievable to him that at one point historians were trying to say that it was Spanish sailors who first settled in this place. What they didn't understand was that the Guaymi Indians were living on the island and then buccaneers from Jamaica came and settled here with many marrying the local Guaymi. This was the hideout for the pirates since it was hard to find coupled with its abundance of fruit and fish. Later on, Spanish sailors came through here. While he was talking to me he pointed to a part of the island with his walking stick. He was making reference to a site where he had taken some British archeologists to where Black buccaneers would make their hunting and fishing tools. "Their tests revealed that the tools I showed them were much older that the date they said Spanish sailors arrived here. Still, there is even more than that they don't understand because I remember my grandparents telling me stories about Africans who were around here many hundred of years ago before any buccaneers or Europeans came here"

Beni`s last point really stuck in my mind as I remembered historian Afua Cooper telling me about the tall African villagers that the Spanish explorers had seen on their arrival in Panama. At this point I was really curious to see what evidence the scientific community in Panama had about this history. With that in mind I headed to the nation's capital Panama City.

After a twelve-hour bus ride I arrived in the capital. It was a beautiful city filled with old Spanish architecture and wide streets. I walked into a record store where I had a wonderful conversation with the owner who was a former record producer. He recounted the painful story of how he had lost all of his master recording tapes when crowds looted his store during the recent American invasion of Panama. The store owner was kind enough to direct me to the Afro -Antillo museum that he told me was the only museum specialising in the history of Panama's Black population.

At the Afro- Antillo museum I met with the curator Juan Rios, who was eager to talk about a subject that he felt had been neglected by scholars in his country. In regard to the presence of Africans in Panama before European arrival, the only documented research he knew of was in the book, "Obras Selectas" by Armanda Fortune. This book researched the African presence in the Darien –which is a region found in Panama's interior. This is the most well know area in terms of a possible early African presence. It was in the Darien that historic records indicate that 1513 the Spanish explorer Balboa traveled with thirty Africans who were long standing residents of that area.

Juan Rios explained to me that before the construction of the Panama Canal, people would settle in the interior of the country. Many places had African names and it was his feeling that another indicator of an African presence was the crop like sugar cane and cotton that could be found in the interior which weren't indigenous to Panama but were to Africa. Additionally there was a definite African influence found in the culinary dishes from the interior. This was borne out when the Miss Universe contest was held in Panama and one of the African contestants upon eating a dish from the interior remarked how similar it was to food from her country.

Juan Rios told me that he was personally aware of other areas where he felt there was a prior African presence. One was in the area around Portobello, another was an area called Las Talbas that was on the way to the interior and where brown skinned people could be found. He also recalled how one day someone had come into the museum and said she had heard from her grandparents that there were Africans on San Miguel Islands before Europeans.

I explained to him that my strategy was to find out the areas that Africans had settled in and then search for possible Black Indian communities. He believed there were many places in Panama where one could find Blakk Indians especially among some of the Aboriginal peoples living in the interior. Later on, my trip I had the opportunity to travel to San Blas Islands, the home of the Kuna Indians. While there I spoke with Ernesto, the grandson of the famous Kuna leader Coleman. He informed me that the mixture of African and Aboriginal people were in many tribes especially the Choco and Bokota. A few Blakk Indians were even pointed out to me among the Kuna population. Listening to the traditional music of the Choco I was struck by the unmistakable African musical influences present in the music.

The link between African and Aboriginal cultures in Panama seemed undeniable.

Panamanian Blakk Indian Children

Peru

Peru

Northern Peru is off the traditional tourist trail but it is an area of considerable historical significance. I visited a town called Zana, the first place in Peru that African slaves had been brought to. The town was heavily influenced by African culture and has a sizable Blakk Indian population.

Almost two hours north of Zana I went to Tucume, where Thor Hyderal, the famed voyageur was currently working. Hyderdal had made various transoceanic voyages using the traditional bolsa boats that were used by ancient African and aboriginal mariners. His objective was to prove that journeys from Africa to South America could have taken place before European arrival on the continent. It is an idea that has generated great controversy. "Pensar que a la navegación pudiera hacerse por negro salvaje en aquellos tiempos es él más completo deliro", commented an early Cuban historian. Translated this means, "To think that this navigation could be done by savage Negroes in this time is be completely delirious".

Yet when I saw the sturdiness and large size of the traditional aboriginal boats as they navigated the very rough Pacific ocean waters off the coast of Peru, there was little doubt in my mind that these or similar vessels could have survived an ocean journey.

A short film "In The Beginning" depicts African explorers arriving on the shores of Turtle Island where they meet aboriginal people and establish a community. The vessel the

Africans arrived in is based on designs traditional to Peruvian balsa boats. The film is loosely based on the historical account of an emperor from Mali Abukar who left Africa with a huge flotilla of ships to explore what lay on the other side of the ocean. He never returned and some historians and scientists feel that his expedition reached North and Central America and met aboriginal people long before Europeans.

Half an hour away from Tucume was the town of Lambayeque, home of the Bruning Museum and some of the most important archeological discoveries in South America. A particularly famous discovery was the tomb of a Moicha King, often referred to as the "Lord of Sipan" who was buried with a large amount of very valuable objects.

One exhibit, which caught my eye, was a gold statue of an unidentified figure. Even though the object was described as being from the ancient Moicha culture it was very much in the style of sculpture that is found in West Africa. In fact, to my eyes, the figure itself was a representation of an African person.

I was reminded of Ivan Sertima's research, published in They Came Before Columbus, on the links between ancient Peru and West Africa. He writes of aboriginal people in Peru sacrificing black sheep in order to procure rain, pointing out that people in West Africa also sacrificed black sheep and black fowls. "Lest it be thought that these are natural choices suggested simply by the colour of the rain clouds," Van Sertima states, "it should be pointed out that the Chinese did the opposite."

Sertima clearly feels that Africans had direct influence on aboriginal people in Peru.

I was curious to hear if any of the staff at the museum had come to any conclusions about the potential connection between Africans and ancient aboriginal cultures in Peru. My queries about this subject prompted one of the researchers at the museum to reveal to me that during one of their excavations they had found a breastplate that they felt was very similar in design to that used by the ancient Egyptians. This comment triggered a discussion about whether Africans, specifically Egyptians, had come to South and Central America. I recounted to the museum staff my own experience that I had at the Jade museum in Costa Rica a few years earlier.

While looking at the museum's exhibits, I had seen a piece of pottery labeled as having "African tripods." The legs of this tripod contained carvings of people's faces whose forehead, lips and other facial features looked like West African people. The director of the museum explained that for many years she had been studying the museum's aboriginal jade collection and had arrived at the conclusion that the pieces were of unmistakably African origins. She showed me a number of designs, ceramics and features of people's faces; all of which she felt were of possible African origins. A carving from the Pacific north coast of Costa Rica had the features and geometrical designs identical to objects found in ancient Egypt.

Inevitably, our conversation at the Bruning Museum turned to the subject of Machu Picchu, which is always discussed when the controversy about a possible Egyptian presence in Peru occurs. The Inca temples at Machu Picchu are probably the most famous archaeological sites in South America. This extremely beautiful city was abandoned for unknown reasons during the early 16 th century. According to the information that has been presented to the rest of the world, the abandoned temples lay hidden for hundreds of years till an American archaeologist "rediscovered" the site in the 1960s. However the fact of the matter is that the local aboriginal people always knew of the existence of Machu Picchu and it was actually a local aboriginal person who showed this American archaeologist where the ancient city was.

My visit to Machu Picchu was a memorable and entertaining because of the presence of an irreverent and sarcastic Inca guide. Extremely proud of his Inca heritage, he nullified the presence of obnoxious European and American tourists with his caustic remarks. Among the targets of his venom was actor Shirley Maclaine. He rolled his eyes and wondered out loud how someone could be so stupid to claim, as she had, that only UFOs could have built the magnificent temples at Machu Picchu. He explained that scientists had proven that the Incas had transported the giant building blocks from a distant quarry. Then, utilizing the same scientific skill that had enabled them to perform brain surgery during this time period, (The Inca often made surgical incisions into the skull to relieve cranial pressure); they had cut and fitted the giant stone blocks together without the benefit of cement. They had done such an incredible job, that temples had survived numerous earthquakes while buildings constructed by the Spanish conquistadors had collapsed.

He also had me rolling on the ground with laughter as he described how an American archaeologist had come across a sun dial which the Inca used to make very advanced and complicated astronomical calculations. However, the archaeologist immediately catalogued the astronomical instrument as something that the Incas used to make corn tortillas! As the guide so clearly put it; this judgment reflected that the mind set of someone who couldn't come to terms with the degree to which Inca society and science had advanced.

As he explained the histories of other aspects of the Machu Picchu ruins, the guide pointed out how the designs of the temples were similar to those of Egyptian pyramids. Like the ancient Egyptians, the Incas had practiced mummification of their dead using similar techniques. What was fascinating for me, however, was the way that he dismissed the possibility of any direct contact between Egyptians and Incas. According to him it was just a sheer coincidence that led to two different cultures, so far apart from one another, to having such clear similarities. This theory of the similarities just being a "coincidence" was one that I would often hear in Peru.

After the tour of Machu Picchu was finished I took the guide aside and spoke with him about research that examined this connection. One of the first things we discussed were the designs of the pyramids. The type of pyramids found in South and Central America is the step pyramid, which can be traced back to ancient Babylon and Egypt, three thousand years before

Christ. One example of step pyramids is the noted Egyptian pyramids of Djoger, at Saggara, built in 2750 BC. There were no pyramids in South and Central America before 800 - 600 BC. This is also the time period that some researchers feel African people had definite contact with aboriginal people in the Americas.

The first step pyramids in the Americas appear at La Venta, also the site that has the statues of colossal heads, which many believe to be of Africans. Other notable step pyramids include the Cerro Colorado pyramids found in the Chicoma valley in northern Peru.

Another important piece of scientific research was a study done by Professor Peulter on embalming mixtures and antiseptic substances used by ancient aboriginal peoples in Peru in their mummification practices. He found this complex, difficult to manufacture formulas were identical to those used in ancient Egypt. These factors make it more difficult to accept the fact that the similarity of the formulas is simply a "sheer coincidence." Needless to say, the guide was intrigued by this information.

At the museum in Paracas, a small town on the southern coast of Peru, I saw some exhibits which provided one of those puzzling potential links to Africa that one often finds in that country. The museum contains various mummies and human remains, which, due to the dry climate, were remarkably preserved. Scientists have been able to learn remarkable things about the health and diseases that affected early inhabitants of this region by studying these skeletal remains. One study, by

T.O. Stewart, demonstrated the presence of a race with a greater average height and a different head shape than the aboriginal people of the area.

This piece of research, which potentially points to an African presence, becomes even more intriguing when one sees the hairstyles that are present on the mummies themselves. Several of the mummies had their head worn in long African-style braids. One of the mummies on display even had dreadlocks that were about four feet long! I asked the museum attendant if this was an accurate representation. He assured me that the dreadlocks I saw were the actual hair of the thousand-year-old mummy. It was believed that the figure was probably a ruler or a medicine person.

I was told similar things at the Bruning Museum in Lambayeque. There, I had seen a replica of a headpiece from the ancient Lambayeque culture. The hair on the piece was plaited in the long braids similar to those found in Africa. I was told that the elite of the Lambayeque culture wore this hairstyle. I had seen photos of a museum exhibit that portrayed ancient aboriginal people in northern Chile, wearing a similar hairstyle. Present day aboriginal people in Chincheros, Peru and also the Chipaya people of Bolivia, still wear their hair in a similar style with several very long braids.

While it is difficult to reach any definite conclusions about these hairstyles one has to admit that their presence, when coupled with archaeological evidence pointing to an early African presence, makes for the intriguing possibility of African hairstyles being adopted by aboriginal peoples.

Travelling north from Paracas, I arrived at the town of Chincha, one of the main centers of modern day Afro-Peruvian culture. When I attended a local fair in Chincha I realized that it was also the location of several Blakk Indian families. I had the opportunity to talk briefly with two families that night. They were very proud of their traditional Afro-Peruvian culture. According to them their community had begun with African slaves that had been brought to Lima. It has been calculated that about 60% of those African slaves were males. At the same time the aboriginal male population were being decimated by the Spanish. Aboriginal women remained in their villages and would often intermarry with the African men.

On a previous journey to Peru, I had the opportunity to witness a performance of the traditional folk music from Chincha. An ensemble of dancers and musicians performed together. The dances were obviously of African origin and it was fascinating for me to see dance movements that were very similar to tap dancing! The musical accompaniment featured a lot of traditional African percussive rhythms. At this particular performance one of the highlights was the incredible skill of a Quechua Indian who played African percussion with the ensemble from Chincha.

The history of Peru has numerous rebellions against unjust regimes and Blakk Indians and Africans have played important roles in some of them.

A conversation I had with Peruvian activist Outra Dub revealed a very interesting link between Africa and Peruvian colonial history. The Spanish conquistador Pizzaro was accompanied by a battalion of Moors (North Africans) named Morochos. The battalion eventually deserted and Pizzaro sent an army after them. They made their last stand at Ayachuco where they were massacred. Out of close to seven hundred Morochos, it is estimated about seventy of them survived. The survivors fled to the Pampas and Congallo where the Quechua Indians took them in. Out of this union developed a community, the "Morochoas".

Juan Santos de Atahuallpa, a man of Incan descent, led several rebellions against the Spanish conquistadors. In the 16 th century part of eastern Peru (the Campa region) remained liberated for many years as a result of his activities. Atahuallpa himself had spent a period of time living and working with priests from Angola. Jesuit priests where he lived and worked had taken Atahuallpa to Angola. Even though it has been documented that he was not free of prejudice against the Black people, Atahuallpas top two generals were of African descent. His fighting force, comprised of Black and First Nations fighters, managed to successfully attack the Spanish.

It was a common practice for rebellious Incas who weren't executed by the Spanish colonialists to be shipped to various parts of Africa including the Spanish Sahara and Angola. This was the case with failed Tupac Amaru rebellion that occurred 1781-3; where Inca nobility suspected of being part of the rebellion was exiled to the Spanish Sahara. The influence of these aboriginal peoples on Africans is something that has not been adequately researched. A parallel example exists with the case of over two hundred Natchez Indians who were shipped to Haiti as punishment for a failed rebellion in Louisiana.

In more recent times, during the late 1960s and 1970s one of the key leaders of the Peruvian guerrilla movement was a Peruvian Blakk Indian named Lobaton. The Ashinak Indians (who inhabit the jungle areas near Iquitos) believed that Lobaton fulfilled one of their prophecies: that a figure would arrive that would deliver them from the colonial oppression they had been subjected to. Their efforts elicited a harsh response from the government who launched a prolonged military onslaught against them and the guerrillas.

As one travels through Peru, one is constantly aware of the on edge, heavily armed, shoot-first-ask-questions-later thugs who call themselves the Peruvian military. They help prop up a fascist regime in a country where the jails are overflowing with political prisoners kept in subhuman conditions. In the meantime, while millions of Peruvians live in abject poverty in the surrounding shantytowns, the idle rich party the night away in affluent suburbs like Miraflores and San Isdro.

Resistance against injustice continues in Peru as some inhabitants work towards a historical moment similar to the successful Pueblo Indian uprising led by the Blakk Indian Pope who successfully drove the Spanish out of the American Southwest in the seventeenth century. While the evidence is uncertain, Pope probably had African as well as aboriginal ancestry. Pope told people that the god Poheyo had come to him during a ceremony at Taos and told him that he had chosen a tall black man as his earthly representative. At that time there was a significant African population in the Southwest.

Ancient Temple

Ancient Indigenous statue from Peru

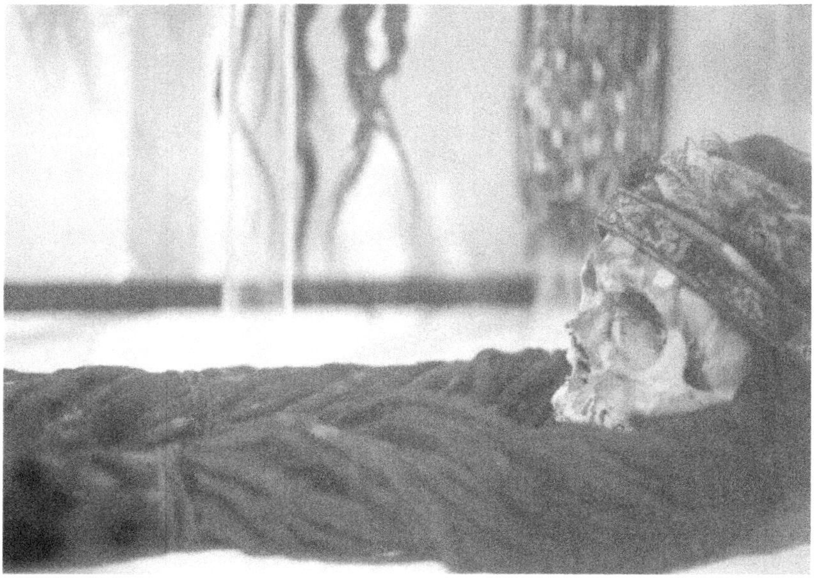

Ancient Indigenous mummy with preserved dreadlocks

Blakk Indian family in Peru

Ecuador

Ecuador

I crossed into Ecuador by taking a bus all along the north coast of Peru. I passed a number of seaside villages and ports in the process including Cabo Blanco where Ernest Hemmingway penned his famous novel "The Old Man and The Sea."

Following a number of time consuming bureaucratic border formalities I was finally allowed entry into Ecuador. Right a way I bordered a bus bound for the capital city Quito, my goal was to reach the Blakk Indian community in Esmeraldas. My destination was literally on the other side of the country by the Colombian border.

After traveling all day I arrived in Quito at 3 am. The air was chilly and after being in the mountains of Peru my body could tell that once again I was at high altitude. (Quito is in fact the second highest capital in South America). I had a two-hour wait before my connecting bus so I purchased some coca tea and passed the time at the bus station, which despite the late hour was teeming with activity. Practically everyone around me was an aboriginal person and most wore traditional dress. I had never seen so many aboriginal men in a major urban center in South America who still wore their traditional clothing. It was a testament to the strength of traditional aboriginal culture in the country. I noticed two or three black people boarding buses heading to Colombia.

Dawn was breaking when my bus connection pulled into the station and soon afterwards I was driving through the

Ecuadorian highlands with its snow capped glacier mountains. As we descended towards the coastal area I noticed more and more Black people on the streets and in the various towns we drove through.

A food stop in a highland town provided me with the sight of Black people walking and working alongside aboriginal people dressed in their traditional clothes. Even though this was something I personally hadn't witnessed often in South America, nobody around me gave this sight a second glance.

The climate and scenery changed dramatically when we entered the province of Esmeraldas with banana (one of the main exports) dominating the landscape in what was now a tropical climate. The majority of people that I saw in the streets were now black. After more than 30 hours of continuous bus travel the bus pulled into Esmeraldas a seaside village near Atacamas.

The reason that I had subjected myself to this arduous journey was because Atacamas was the site where in the late 16 th century a vessel arrived with hundreds of Africans slaves bound for Peru. The Africans on board broke out, overpowered and killed all the Europeans on the ship. The Africans proceeded to establish a maroon republic in Esmeraldas. In the 1580's Miguel Cabello Balboa wrote about this republic detailing how the republic was primarily Blakk Indian because the liberated Africans who were predominantly males had taken aboriginal women as their wives.

Today Esmeraldas is a region with a lot of poverty and with people preoccupied with hustling the foreign tourists who come for the local beaches. While it was obvious looking at the faces of the local people that most were Blakk Indian there really wasn't anything commemorating that this was the site of what used to be a very noteworthy maroon republic. If I hadn't been previously aware of the history I would never have guessed the significance of this area. My inquiries yielded little information about the Blakk Indian histories here.

I did manage to have a conversation with some Colombians who told me that their country west full of Blakk Indian people especially along the coast. They felt Colombia was the place I should visit. My own research had shown me that Colombia and Venezuela were countries that had large Blakk Indian populations due to the numerous maroon communities that were established in these countries. Blakk Indian rebels acquired a lot of notoriety especially in Venezuela where their outlaw activities became the subject of correspondence by the King of Spain.

I decided to make my way to Colombia since I really wasn't far from the Colombian border.

Colombia

Colombia

While I was able to make it to Colombia my travel was restricted by government troop and paramilitary activity. Still I was about to meet with activists from the Colombian Movement of communities of African Descendent.

These Afro Colombians are direct descendants of African slaves who formed communities along the riverbanks of Colombia's interior. Over hundreds of years the Afro Colombians have maintained a lot of their traditional African cultural ties and this is very evident in their rich traditional music, with its obvious debt to African percussive rhythms. Many Afro Colombian communities are in close proximity to aboriginal communities and certainly over the years there has been cultural exchange and intermarriage between the two groups. It was the political alliance between these two groups that impressed me the most.

Like numerous aboriginal communities, Afro Colombians occupy lands rich in minerals and medicinal plants. Multinationals especially pharmaceutical companies have been attempting to enter these territories in order to exploit the minerals and plant life there. Pharmaceutical companies have been pursuing the strategy of finding out which plants are used by indigenous peoples for medicinal use. Afterwards they return to Europe and North America and put patents on these medicines and plants and begin to sell them commercially. This has happened in Bolivia where American companies have registered patents in North America for Bolivian grains like quinoa, which have been used by aboriginal people in Bolivia for thousands of years. These companies then attempt to prevent Bolivians selling their products containing quinoa because they now "own" the patent.

Multinationals in Colombia were trying to do whatever they could to enter into agreements with individual aboriginal tribes to exploit the resources in their territories. These companies even went as far as to support aboriginal demands for sovereignty. Their motivation in doing so was certainly not out of respect for the legitimate rights that should be accorded to aboriginal peoples. Instead multinationals felt that it would be to their advantage to sign agreements with individual aboriginal tribes than with the government of Colombia. It was their view that compared to the Colombian government individual aboriginal tribes would have less resources and international legal options to defend themselves if the multinationals broke any agreements they entered into.

Like other aboriginal peoples in Colombia, the Afro Colombians were battling for recognition of their right to the territory they inhabitant. After a struggle they had received some recognition of their rights from the Colombian government at the same time they astutely realized the maneuvers that the multinationals were attempting to use against them.

The Afro Colombians were joining with their aboriginal neighbors to combat the multinationals. Contrary to a growing international stereotype of aboriginal people from South

America as being simplistic people always in need of guidance and direction from European or American activists or "philanthropic" rock stars, the Afro Colombians had developed their own strategies to combat multinational interests.

When I spoke with the Afro Colombians I found they had developed sophisticated strategies and policies on issues like intellectual property rights, international patents, genetic farming to name a few. In fact the Afro Colombians were in contact with and working with farmers in India that were taking radical action against multinational genetic farms that were destroying their traditional farming.

The Afro Colombians and aboriginals had both realized that in the twenty first century the fight for the survival of their peoples and their culture would involve struggle on new battleground and in an impressive manner they were preparing for that!

Bolivia

Bolivia

The landscape of the Yungas is immense and spectacular. A typical scene is one in which a waterfall gushes from steep mountains shrouded in mist. The power of the landscape is felt immediately. The further one descends into the valleys of the Yungas the more tropical the vegetation becomes, one can see the mangoes and the green terraced fields on which coca is grown.

When I first visited Bolivia in 1992, I was shown a postcard with a picture of the people of the Yungas. Superficially, the photo looked like that of a black woman dressed in the clothing typically worn by many Quechua Indian woman today. Many present day Quechua women wear clothing that were imposed on them by the Spanish conquistadors. This typically consists of voluminous skirts with bowler-type hats worn with their hair in two large plaits tied together at the back.

Looking at that photograph, I realized the possibility of there being a Blakk Indian community in Bolivia. After further inquiry I was told that these women were the descendants of African slaves that the Spanish had brought to work the silver mines and plantations in Bolivia. When the slaves had obtained their freedom, many chose to live in the subtropical region of the Yungas where they intermarried with the indigenous people of the area.

As I journeyed into this region I kept looking for signs of Blakk Indians. Occasionally as the bus drove along I would sight a few black faces far off in the distance, but no sign of a Black

Indian community. After five hours of traveling, the bus stopped in a small village. A friend had told me about a town in the Yungas that they thought would be important in terms of my finding a Blakk Indian community. As it got darker, I walked to one of the food stands and inquired if there were buses heading to this town. The person at the stand immediately pointed to a huge open truck, filled with people carrying their various goods. It was in the process of pulling out so I made a quick decision to jump on board. I had to scramble down a hill and grab onto the truck's railing until I was safe on a sideboard. From there I had a clear view of the truck's interior. It was crammed with people, crates of produce, animals and furniture. I spied a small, empty space on the floorboard where I thought I would be able to stand. I took aim and jumped from the top of the truck, managing to land perfectly between the two crates. My efforts were awarded with applause from the passengers.

Soon the truck was hurtling along. Occasionally we had to duck to avoid being hurt by the tall trees that lined the road. Suddenly there was a flurry of rain and hail.

All the passengers had to work together to cover the back of the truck with tarpaulin. This proved to be a source of excitement and laughter as the people skidded around the wet bus trying to fix the tarpaulin on to keep their goods and produce dry. While the majority of passengers on the truck were Quechua Indian people there were a group of five Blakk Indian women. Their features astounded me because they reminded me so much of people I had seen on previous trips to Africa.

After an hour and a half of traveling, we arrived in a small town. I was greeted by a number of young Blakk Indian children peering at me from a hillside and pointing at my dreadlocks. As I walked along the town's dirt road I could also see Quechua Indian women some of whom had babies slung over their shoulders in blankets.

I had originally planned to return to La Paz later that night, but my plans changed when I found out that there were no other buses leaving until six a.m. the next morning. There were also no hotels in the town since this was not an area open to tourists. The bus driver suggested that I sleep in the back of the bus until he was ready to leave the next morning but I decided to keep walking to check out the rest of the town. It was situated on the edge of a mountaintop with breathtaking views of coca fields and the surrounding mountains.

The main road was lined with small houses and an occasional shop. Very soon I was surrounded by two Blakk Indian women and at least a dozen children all of whom were curious about my dreadlocks.

This group of people really caught my attention. They had an incredible variety of facial features and were all different shades of brown and black. I had never seen a people who looked quite like this. The two women confirmed that indeed many of the families were Blakk Indian. They also pointed out a house further down the road where I might sleep.

A Blakk Indian couple owned the house. It was a very simple dwelling with an extra cot on the upper level and a front section out of which produce was sold. I noticed there was a calendar in the house, which had "COCA IS NOT COCAINE", printed in big bold letters. One of the owners informed me that he was a coca farmer and wanted to know what information I had about coca. I explained that I understood coca to have many medicinal properties, that it was good for asthma, arthritis, and stomach problems but most people believed in the myth that it was the same as cocaine. Reassured by my attitude, the man invited me to sit down at their table for tea and some conversation. Beside our table there was a gigantic crocus bag filled with at least forty pounds of coca leaf. The couple took a handful of leaves from the bag and placed them in a pot of hot water. They let the leaves seep for a while to make a refreshing pot of coca tea. We sat a while drinking coca tea and chatting.

Certainly it was clear to me that one of the most important things that forcibly transplanted Africans learned, from the aboriginal people in Bolivia was how to cultivate and utilize coca.

While we were talking I was asked if I had ever heard saya music. He told me that he had a live recording by a friend of his, a well know saya musician. He got the cassette from his bedroom and played it for me. He explained that saya music was a form of Blakk Indian music that had originated in the Yungas. It utilizes a combination of Andean instrumentation with African percussion. The percussive elements reminded me of music that I had heard in Cuba and Haiti, but there were also musical elements present which are unique to the aboriginal people of Bolivia. He explained that the performer Daniel Barra was presently performing in another region of Bolivia but he thought it would be good for me to speak with him. As I left the village at six a.m. that morning, I decided I would return in the future to meet with Daniel Barra.

It took me a year and a half, but I did make it back to the Yungas. On my return journey I had a direct brush with the legendary avalanches that have acted as a deterrent to many travelers. The dangerously narrow and precipitous roads of the Yungas are often marked with crosses decorated with flowers that commemorate motorists who have careened off the narrow roads into the treacherous ravines of the Yungas.

Halfway through the journey, the bus I was traveling on stopped. Ahead of us I could see that two other buses had stopped with the majority of their passengers standing on the roadside staring and pointing to the mountains above. The reason for their attention soon became obvious. Giant boulders were plunging off the mountain and bouncing off the road ahead. It was explained to me that because of melting snow on top of the mountain, avalanches were occurring. For about an hour and a half everybody stood around watching as giant boulders intermittently crashed down from the side of the mountain. All of a sudden without any warning the drivers of all the buses including the one I was traveling on, gunned their engines and raced through the dangerous section of the road. Apparently they were accustomed to this and didn't want to be thrown too much off their schedule. There were about thirty passengers who, like myself, were still standing on the roadside when the buses took off. We now had to run for about two hundred yards through this dangerous section of the road to rejoin our buses. We ran as quickly as possible, trying to keep as close to the mountain side as we could. Luckily for us only a couple of smaller boulders bounced harmlessly over our heads and we were able to safely make it to where our buses were waiting for us.

Afterwards the very relieved passengers worked off the nervous tension with numerous jokes and anecdotes about our run through the avalanche. Thankfully, our journey continued without any further incident.

I arrived at my destination in the late afternoon and was immediately greeted by several residents of the town who walked with me until I got to the small house on the hillside where Daniel Barra lived. In his early forties, Daniel was very happy to show me the instruments that he and his family used to perform saya. He brought out a range of percussive instruments: gourds, drums, shakers and rattles that were attached to the performer's ankles when they danced. The primary instruments were drums made from designs passed on from their African slave ancestors. There were also various instruments that were used by Quechua Indian people. Daniel explained to me that at saya's base were the rhythms that their African ancestors played when they were slaves in Bolivia. They then incorporated instrumentation that they learnt from Quechua Indian people living in Bolivia.

Now in the Yungas they were making an effort to maintain their African culture by having African cultural classes for the young people. He introduced to me one of his young relatives who was one of the lead vocalists in his group.

Although only six years old, she already knew many of the traditional saya songs and dance movements, all of which had their origins in the dances African slaves used to perform. Relaxed and with great self-confidence, she started singing and dancing, accompanied on percussion by her uncle. A crowd of people from the community gathered around to listen to her. Afterwards, it was touching to see that the young children who were present were so appreciative and protective of their young, talented friend. Her performance made the long journey all that more worthwhile and I left the town realizing that I had been graced with a rare insight into saya, a very unique form of Blakk Indian music.

Blakk Indian children in village

Young Saya music singer

Blakk Indians cultivating coca

Chile

Chile

Chile is not a country that most people associate with having a Black population much less a Blakk Indian one. Yet I traveled to the desert region of northern Chile in search of Blakk Indians. I was acting on two pieces of ancient oral information I had received. The first was of stories of black men coming from Peru across the Andes. The second came from a Chilean who had told me that there would be Blakk Indians in this area because of old stories they had heard about black people trying to cross this section of the mountains but finding it too difficult, with many perishing while trying. While I had no way of verifying this information I felt it was worthwhile to make the journey to check it out. The terrain of this region makes a difficult one to survive in. Immense mountains and snow-capped volcanoes dominate this very raw and arid almost surreal landscape. The cactus that is prevalent in this area are a unique species; thin like candlesticks the arms of these cactus point downward instead of upwards like most cacti. The result is that they appear to be like giant chandeliers.

After trekking through the spectacularly immense mountains and canyons I ended up in the northern town of Arica. Walking the streets in search of a hotel, I passed several Blakk Indians. I ended up chatting with one of them, a municipal worker named Pedro de Bravo. I asked him about his ancestral roots. He revealed that his mother was black and that his black grandfather had married an aboriginal woman from the

Altiplano. Pedro had been trying to find out more information about the aboriginal side of his family but no one in his family wanted to speak about it.

Many writers have remarked on the "silencing" and denial of African heritage within South and Central America historical writing. A Chilean woman named Andrea recounted to me how her own family did not want to acknowledge their African and aboriginal ancestry. Her family was so ashamed of her cousin's kinky hair that they made her shave her head so that people couldn't see her hair and make the connection to her African ancestry. In Andrea's opinion these actions were a by-product of colonialism still in effect.

In a parallel vein, in Chile there is a widespread denial amongst much of the population of their aboriginal ancestry. Many people like to claim European ancestry no matter how distant it may be. Time and time again in my travels in Chile, I would be speaking with someone of very obvious aboriginal ancestry, but when I asked them about their family background they, would go on and on about all the relatives and ancestors they had in Spain and Germany. Ironically, a Chilean sociologist told me that the majority of Chileans had aboriginal ancestry. As well, Chile is the home to the Mapuche people, one of the largest and oldest groups of aboriginal people in South America. Known for the resistance they put up against the Spanish Conquistadors, who, like the Incas before them, were unable to conquer the Mapuche people. The Mapuche are still putting up massive resistance today against the Chilean government and their attempts to log and construct dams on Mapuche territory.

I related some of these incidents to Pedro de Bravo. He concurred there was a heavy colonial mentality amongst Chilean people. This had hindered his own personal search for the history of black people in Chile. It had been incredibly difficult to find historical information on black people in Chile and consequently he felt I would face a formidable task researching Blakk Indian histories.

These histories exist in Chile but I found it's not easy to uncover them.

Brasil

Brasil

From Santa Cruz in Bolivia I got on the "train of death" for the twenty-four hour train ride to the Brasilian frontier. It had earned its nickname because of the train's propensity to plunge off its tracks. As well, it was a favorite target for thieves who would rob passengers, strip them of all their clothes and throw them off the train into the jungle. I was on this train since there was flooding at this time of year there were no options in terms of buses and other vehicles and the cost of flights was too prohibitive.

It was easy to see why the train was a favorite among thieves. As soon as darkness fell it was pitch black in the over crowded train which was constantly making stops in the jungle at small communities. I had to make sure that I stayed awake and alert for the duration of the trip.

During the train ride, I had plenty of opportunity to think about the history of Brasil and some of the potential Blakk Indian links. One of the issues I pondered was Jack Forbes's research indicating that many of the slaves that the Dutch had sold in the French Caribbean Islands were aboriginal people from Brasil. In 1656, some twenty Brasilian slaves were used to suppress an Angolan rebellion in Guadeloupe. Dutch military expeditions to Africa utilized a significant number of aboriginal people from Brasil (especially Tupi and Tupaya Indians) as auxiliary soldiers. They were used in successful expeditions against Portuguese forts along the Gold Coast (1637-38), the Angolan forts of Ano

Bom and Soa Tome as well as the capture of Axum in Guinea. The force used in the expedition against Ano Bom and Soa Tome contained 240 Tupi soldiers.

Today there is still evidence of a Tapuya influence in Elmina Ghana. The Tupaya people remained in Ghana since if they returned to Brasil their Portuguese enemy would have killed them. Their descendants who have married into the local Ghanaian population can be found living in towns like Posto Novo, Why Dah and Grand Pope.

Rebellious aboriginal people from the Ceara region of Brasil were sent to Angola. Other locations in Africa where aboriginal people where shipped to include: Cabo Verde Islands, Azores, Soa Tome.

An important area of research that needs to be pursued is to study the aboriginal influence on modern day African culture.

The long train trip through the jungle took me to Corumba, Brasil. What struck me right away was the incredible variety of racial mixtures present in the population. My Brasilian friend Tanan told me that most people in Brasil are a mix of African, Aboriginal and Portuguese. This was a reflection of the fact that the Portuguese colonialists mixed with the African and aboriginal population in the country.

In 1869 the French minister to Brasil Count de Gobineau wrote "there is no longer a Brasilian family that has no Negro and Indian blood in its vein". For example I saw people who had kinky Afro style hair, which is typical of black people who at the same time had thin slanted eyelids characteristic of aboriginal people in the area. Later when I arrived in Pernambuco it was explained to me by my host Dr. Carricone that in Brasil a term for Blakk Indians was Cafuso.

Anthropologist Richard Price's Maroon Societies speaks of another set of Blakk Indians in Brasil who were called Cabores. This union had occurred when escaped African slaves had come together with aboriginal people. In Brasil escaped slaves often established self-sufficient resistance communities called Quilumbos. They obtained their food by fishing and hunting and cultivating various types of beans, manioc and sweet potatoes. Portuguese colonial records describe a quilumbo at Sao Vincent that was captured as containing "six Negroes, eight Indian men, nineteen Indian women, ten male Cabores and eleven female Cabores". The largest and longest-surviving quilumbo was located in the province of Pernambuco at a site called Palmares. Palmares was a maroon republic that has achieved legendary status by being the longest surviving quilumbo. It was founded at the start of the 17 th century. Palmares was a large well-organised community presided over by an African style court of justice. It was self sufficient in food due to the large crops that were planted and harvested by the community who utilized African irrigation methods. A visitor to Palmares in 1640 estimated 11 thousand people were living there. After 1657 the Dutch decided that Palmares was a threat that had to be destroyed and began an intense military campaign against the quilumbo. Palmares responded with the use of brilliant military tactics and strategies including an African tactic of digging large pits, which were filled with upright sharpened spears. These pits were covered with grass and were next to impossible to detect resulting in a painful death to enemy troops who fell in.

The Portuguese made numerous efforts to destroy this famous resistance settlement. A report from an expedition led by Rilexo Barro provides some interesting indicators of the Blakk Indian presence in this settlement. His report states, "one-hundred Negroes of Palmares were killed. One force captured thirty-one defenders including seven Indians and some mulatto children". It is important to note that the term "mulatto" was originally used in the Americas to refer to the offspring of aboriginal and African parents. Only later was it used to refer to the children of African and European parents.

Speaking with Veronica Gomes, the Co-ordinator of the Ojumbay center, an Afro-Brasilian non-governmental organization in Olinda, I was provided with further insights into the history of quilumbos in Brasil. While previously there had been no recognition for the resistance fighters of the quilumbos like Zumbi who fought against the Portuguese, Ms Gomes was highly critical of the current representations of the quilumbos. She told me that both a 1964 film and a 1996 television miniseries entitled "Zumbi" were full of inaccuracies (especially in regards to the portrayal of Zumbi) and that they neglected to mention the involvement of aboriginal communities. Despite this, some interesting information was uncovered during the production of the miniseries. A linguist was hired to reconstruct the language spoken in the quilumbos. It became apparent that the reconstructed language was a mixture of African, aboriginal and Portuguese. Like the language of modern day Brasil, Ms Gomes felt the union of African and aboriginal people were very much reflected in the Brasilian language. Also, she indicated that a professor from Sao Paulo had recently done an archeological survey of the quilumbos at Palmares. Among the finds was a set of clay pipes that were typical of those used by aboriginal people in Brasil.

While visiting the Centro Nordesta Popular Medicino, a center specializing in herbal medicine in Recife, I met Mrs. Santana. At first I assumed that she was a Black woman, her features were those I had seen in numerous Brasilians. She corrected me by saying "I am Cafuso". It was a telling moment for me as I realized that assessing people's ancestry in Brasil wouldn't be the easiest task. After that I got into the habit of specifically asking Brasilians their ancestry when I met them.

As I traveled further north in the state of Maranho where there was a greater proximity to aboriginal populations, I could clearly see the mix between black and aboriginal. This was also true in parts of the state of Bahia, the entry point of African slaves into Brasil, especially around the villages of Arrail d'Ajuda and Caravia. They also happened to be located near small aboriginal reserves.

In the 16 th century aboriginal people in Bahia captured a European slave ship coming from Soa Tome in Africa. They liberated the African slaves on board and free Blakk Indian communities were established as a result.

The Blakk Indian cultural link can also be found in Brasilian music. My first experience of this was when I witnessed a performance of maracatu music in the city of Olinda in Pernambuco state. It was in the weeks just preceding carnival and various bands were having practice sessions in the streets. One day I just happened to be walking and suddenly in front of me was a procession of musicians and dancers closely followed by a jubilant dancing crowd.

The musicians used trumpets and other brass instruments accompanied by a variety of drums. Tanan Cariconde, a musician from Olinda, explained to me that Maracatu music utilized a lot of African rhythms. This was apparent from the musical patterns being played on the bass drums. There was also a heavy aboriginal influence to maracatu and this was reflected particularly in the cadence of the music. A possible origin of the Blakk Indian connection in this music is when African slaves from Guinea and Angola were put to work in the fields alongside aboriginal people from Brasil. In the same way that blues music in the USA was influenced by some of the melodies that African slaves working in the fields learned from their aboriginal co-workers; I feel that this might have also occurred in Brasil.

The dancing that accompanies maracatu provides clear indicators of the influence of both African and aboriginal people. Dancers alternate between doing aboriginal dance steps (specific to the Amazon regions of Brasil), which resemble synchronized swaying movements and jig like movements that are obviously of African origin. It is common to see performers dressed to represent African royalty.

An aboriginal influence is also clear with many dancers carrying spears and wearing headdresses made out of coconut boughs, which in Brasil is a signifier of indigenous culture.

There is a specific group called caboclinhos who each year participate in carnival dressed in aboriginal regalia. This caboclinhos tradition is a very important one in Olinda and Recife carnivals and I was told that sometimes members of Pernambucos aboriginal population participate in these groups. One aboriginal group that does participate is the Fulni-o from Agua Belas. I had the opportunity to listen to a CD "cantando com sol" that was recorded by some singers from their community. The groups' producer Boro explained to me that there was a specific type of music "samba de coca" that had started when the Fulni-o people had gotten together with African runaway slaves who inhabited a nearby quilombo. The story goes that this musical form was born when after drinking some coconut water the two people started using the empty coconut shells as percussion instruments and started singing to the rhythms they pounded out using the empty coconut shells.

In a similar manner the Blakk Indian cultural mix can also be heard in bumbu boi a traditional music found in the state of Maranhao. While I was there I was told about a unique village called Curiau. Located in Northern Brasil, the inhabitants are descendants of African slaves who maintained the customs of their ancestors. It was explained to me that they were most likely related to the Bush Negroes of Surinam, whose ancestors were escaped African slaves who intermarried with aboriginal inhabitants of Surinam. They established numerous successful Maroon communities in Surinam.

When I later arrived in Belem I headed to the archival center of the city. There I found a variety of old documents that detailed the presence of various quilombos that were formed by runaway African slaves. These slaves had been brought to the Amazon to be used in tasks like the collection of rubber and the harvesting of timber after plantation owners were unsatisfied with the low productivity of aboriginal slaves. In a variety of instances, these African slaves especially in the Macapa region, escaped and together with the local aboriginal population established new communities that were one of the sources of the very significant blakk Indian population present today. After slavery was abolished it was also common for freed black slaves seeking to escape the city to end up in remote locations close to aboriginal communities. In some cases links were formed due to trading between the two groups and in some instances intermarriage resulted. As I watched the fishing boats being unloaded by a number of Blakk Indians in the main market in Belem (the enormous" ver-o peso" market) I realized how with the importance the river boat travel in this region that this had also greatly facilitated the mixing of black and aboriginal people as black people moved around the waterways of the region working on fishing vessels.

* * *

One day at Zumbi music, a music stall which sold only vinyl releases on the street of Rio de Janeiro, I came across a recording of folkloric music from the south of Brasil. At the time I was actually searching for traditional music from the Nordeste where there are a large number of Blakk Indian people. I was especially hoping to see if I could find recordings of the Kairiri Xocu; a Blakk Indian tribe living in the urban areas of Porto Real de Coleigo in the Nordeste. Instead I found this recording entitled "traditional music of Rio Grande de Sul" (the southern most state of Brasil which borders Uruguay). Inside the album were extensive liner notes and photos of the performers. I was surprised to see most of the performers were black. Throughout my travels in Brasil I had been constantly told that black people were practically non-existent in the more European influenced south of Brasil. I became even more curious about the south when I saw that there were a series of tracks, which were titled "music inspired by indigenous people". According to the liner notes this was music made by people who had studied aboriginal instrumentation and songs. Using aboriginal instruments they made music that was inspired by their respect for aboriginal people and their way of life. Having not found information in books on this I realized that I would have to travel to the south.

After forty hours on the bus I arrived in Porto Alegre the capital of Rio Grand de Sul. As I walked around in the commercial center of the city not only did I see Aboriginal people selling handicrafts on the street corners but I also saw numerous black people walking around. Several people I passed

I identified as Blakk Indian people. Exhausted I sat down on a park bench to rest. Soon afterwards a black man sat down beside me and we started talking. He explained he was a musician in a local band and he was just starting to get involved with learning about social issues. He asked if I was doing anything at the moment, and invited me to come to a meeting he was on his way to. From there we headed up the street towards the meeting.

When I entered the meeting room I found that it was full of black people who were artists, musicians, dancers and historians who were having a planning session for a cultural event coming up. Speaking with the director of a black dance company she explained to me that most of the time when her dancers performed in other parts of Brasil they had a hard time convincing people they were from the south because of this mythology that black people don't exist there. She agreed with my assertion that there are a number of Black Indians living in the south.

The next day I had the opportunity to speak with two students of the Brasilian martial arts form called Caporeira Angola. They were well versed in the history of black people in the south and they shared their knowledge with me. In the early 1800s these fugitive slaves lived in a quilombo located in what is now known as Cidade Baixa. A special police force called capitana de matas was established just to hunt fugitive slaves.

In one of his songs entitled "Arreal de Baronesa" a prominent black musician from Porto Allegre; Giba Giba sings about what is regarded as most likely the site of the first quilombo in the south a location called Menino Deus. At the time of Brasil's war with Paraguay many blacks fought in the war after they were promised liberty if they did so. Instead of liberty they were rewarded with executions. Other black slaves who fought made their way into Uruguay, Paraguay and Argentina where some of their descendants live today. The black slaves in this war were used like fodder and placed at the front of the battle lines where they suffered the highest causalities. After the abolition of slavery in 1888 the black population of Porto Alegre became centered in cidade Baixa where they lived with other marginalized people.

Near the sites of the quilombos where fugitive black slaves were areas inhabited by the local aboriginal population. For example near the quilombo at Menino Deus is an area called Mouro Osso where aboriginal people lived.

Speculation about Blakk Indian history in the south is that the proximity of fugitive black slaves and aboriginal communities (along with the trading that existed between the two communities) gave birth to present day Blakk Indians found in Rio Grand de Sul.

The question of a modern day Blakk Indian identity in Brasil is not something from my perception at the forefront of the minds of the country's population.

I have often wondered why public expression of pride in one's Blakk Indian ancestry was so uncommon in Brasil. Certainly one of the reasons for this can be traced to contemporary Brasilian attitudes to their aboriginal ancestry and people in general. This segment of the Brasilian population is completely marginalized and for the most part rendered invisible especially in terms of media representation. The main exception being around Carnival time where a multitude of people dress in costumes with an obvious aboriginal influence. Popular conceptions of indigenous people have them living only in the Amazon and Mato Grosso regions. The majority of residents in Brasil's largest city São Paulo (one of the largest cities in the world) are unaware of the fact that there are aboriginal communities i.e. Guarani Indians existing in conditions of great poverty on the outskirts of the city and within the city's favelas (ghettoes).

As one Brasilian pointed out to me the majority of Brasilians have some aboriginal ancestry yet when they fill in census forms they don't acknowledge this. They are likely to acknowledge their African or European ancestry. Education and public consciousness has focused more in reclaiming pride in Brasil's African heritage.

Even legislature providing protection against acts of racism has in the past neglected to specifically protect aboriginal people. The legislation has contained more specific points to protect black people in Brasil. In 1998 while I was in the city of Brasilia there was the case of an aboriginal man Galdino who had come to the city to attend a meeting about aboriginal rights; unable to find a hotel he went to sleep on a sidewalk. The teenage sons of wealthy local politicians and judges poured gasoline over the sleeping man and lit him on fire. The aboriginal man died from his burns. In a statement one of the offenders admitted his guilt but in his defense claimed that he didn't know it was an aboriginal man, he thought it was a homeless person. The fact that despite admitting his guilt he received a very light punishment (many feel if there hadn't been a media spotlight on the case he would have gotten off Scot-free.). What transpired in this case speaks volumes about the attitudes towards the poor and aboriginal people in Brasil.

The most astute comment I have heard from a Brasilian describing the political situation of aboriginal people in Brasil came from Marcello Yuka, founder of the band O'Rappa: "the treatment aboriginal people receive is a reflection of the power they are perceived to have. Since they are perceived as insignificant, powerless people in the minds of politicians; this is used as a justification for the abysmal treatment they receive in the political landscape."

* * *

One day while walking the streets of Salvador, I saw a black woman who was selling a variety of religious objects. I immediately noticed that one of the objects for sale was a statue of an aboriginal man wearing a headdress. The vendor explained that the statues were used for purposes of protection by followers of the Afro Brasilian religion Umbanda. Having seen similar statues in the households of Santeria in Santiago, Cuba I knew right away that this pointed to a Blakk Indian spiritual link.

Some time later in the city of Sao Paulo I was attending a performance by an Afro Brasilian dance company. Unlike, similar companies, they included an interpretation of Umbanda. As part of the theatrical presentation they had an authority on Umbanda planted in the audience who answered questions posed by the cast members about the religion. After the performance, I asked him some questions about the significance of aboriginal spirits in Umbanda. He introduced himself as Pai Sydney de Xango, a high priest of Umbanda. We had a great conversation and he paid great attention to the links I was able to point out to him between aboriginal people and voodoo in Haiti. As a result of our conversation he invited me to an Umbanda ceremony that would be held at his family's house.

The next week I arrived at his house at midnight. From outside the house I could hear the sound of African drumming and singing. I was ushered into a large room where the Umbanda ceremony was occurring. I was greeted by Pai Sydney de Xango who was directing a group of white clad participants as they danced and chanted around large ceremonial objects in the room to the sound of African rhythms provided by a group of percussionists. As I looked around I noticed that in one corner room was a statue of a black woman wearing the traditional white Umbanda clothing. In the other corner was a statue of an aboriginal man wearing a headdress. Hanging from the ceiling was a pot filled with feathers and feathers were also attached to an object hanging from one of the walls. I knew enough about the religious symbolism to understand that these feathers were representing a spiritual connection with the spirits of the aboriginal ancestors of Brasil. Pai Sydney conducted the ceremony in the West African language of Yoruba. At various points in the ceremony different spirits possessed the participants. Their entire demeanor was transformed as they danced possessed under the careful guidance of Pai Sydney and his assistants who took them through various rituals. Homage was paid to various African gods (Orixas) and participants would come out dressed in various incredible costumes and masks to represent specific Orixas. Throughout the ceremony the energy in the room was electric. There was non-stop drumming and chanting and the graceful movements of Pai Sydney as he danced while chanting prayers and incantations in Yoruba. At one point in the ceremony a young boy who was about nine years old, wearing only white pants and with the rest of his body painted with white dots was given the spotlight of the ceremony as only he and Pai Sydney danced around the room. The young boy danced using traditional Yoruba moves singing incantations until he went into a state of trance. This was a major step for the young boy and all who were present gave him applause for his efforts.

When the ceremony finished at four that morning, pots of traditional Bahian and Nigerian cooking were brought out and all the participants and their guests and relatives were served by Pai Sydney and his assistants. Afterwards people hung out and socialized. While waiting to speak with Pai Sydney I spoke with one of the participants who turned out to be the aunt of the young boy who had been dancing in the ceremony. She informed me that this night marked the eighteenth anniversary of her coming to Umbanda. She also revealed to me that her father was aboriginal and her mother was African.

After the food was consumed, I had a chance to speak with Pai Sydney. He explained to me that in the late nineteenth century Allan Kardec brought a form of spiritualism to Brasil. Allan Kardec was a French writer who in the nineteenth century wrote several books on spiritualism and mediums. These books reached Brasil and groups were started which were based on this writing, giving rise to the movement known as Kardecismo. This spiritualism had its origin in Europe and was very Euro centric. At some point in the 1870s followers of Kardenismo were having a séance when an aboriginal spirit tried to come into the session but the white practitioners wouldn't let it enter. The aboriginal spirit said that a new religion should be formed that would respect and incorporate the spirits of Black and aboriginal ancestors. The first Umbanda house was established in Recife during the 1870s and was called "tenda de umbanda do caboclo das sete enctuzilhados".

One of the tenets which distinguish Umbanda with other Afro Brasilian religions such as Candomble is the space and respect that it gives to the aboriginal spirits known as Cabocle. (I should point out that I was told that possibly a very early form of Candomble' called Candomble d' Angola might have had aboriginal spiritual links but this is a very difficult area to research). There are various aboriginal spirits in Umbanda such as Iron Chest, White Feathers, and Seven Arrows. As Pai Sydney told me, often on the altars at Umbanda temples you will see aboriginal statues and feathers that signify those spirits. I didn't witness this at this particular ceremony, but I have been informed that there are Umbanda ceremonies that invoke the aboriginal spirits who speak through the devotees and suggest potions and incantations for those with medical problems. He also explained to me that Umbanda wanted to respect and honor the spirits of the ancestors of the aboriginal people of Brasil, on whose land they were. This was the reason that there was a statue of the aboriginal man in the corner of the room as one enters. While it was clear to me that the focus of Umbanda was on its traditional African roots, its practitioners went out of their way to honor the aboriginal presence and spirits in their ceremonies. One aboriginal observer who was present at the ceremony commented to me that if Europeans had shown this type of respect for aboriginal culture when they arrived in Brasil, perhaps the devastation of aboriginal people in Brasil wouldn't have occurred.

Brasilian carnival float in Rio

Brasilian carnival float in Rio

Brasilian Umbanda statue

Brasilian: Blakk Indian in Belem

Marcelo "Troublemaker" Yuka

Exploring Spiritual Connections

Exploring Spiritual Connections

A common point that doesn't seem to have provoked much dispute is the fact that Africans and Aboriginal people, upon first contact, discovered that they shared a spiritual outlook that had many parallels. Certainly key to this was the shared belief in the spirit world. This is a point that resonates on a personal level for me. I remember vividly one of the first conversations that I had with Jeannette Armstrong, Okanagan Indian writer and educator; one of our first point of agreement was when she said to me, "they try to tell us the spirit world doesn't exist that the spirits don't exist, but we know they are there, we see them."

This mutual recognition of the spirit world by some black and aboriginal people was brought home to me in an episode that was recounted to me years ago. An aboriginal activist had been jailed and his immediate family was worried about him. They consulted a medicine person, who transformed into a coyote and appeared in the prison to see what was occurring with this family member. According to the activist, when the coyote appeared, it was as if time was frozen momentarily and then the coyote disappeared. It happened to be suppertime when this occurred, even though numerous inmates were around at the time, not one of them saw or commented on the appearance of the coyote. However, the aboriginal activist said right afterwards a sole Black inmate approached him with a scared look in his eyes and said, "did you see that coyote?". Talking with him further, he discovered that this inmate's grandmother practiced a traditional African religion.

Intrigued by this event, and pondering its significance; I went and visited with my close friend Pineshi Gustin, who is a keeper of traditional Ojibway ways. I recounted the episode to her and she had the following response for me:

"As a child, I learnt from the elders that we are born in the world but the realities are not split off like we would think. They believe the spirit world and this world are in sync, that there is no separation –so when that incident happened to your friend and this other Black guy, they were operating on the same level and they tuned out the reality as it exists right now –this dense thing –and slip into the spirit world –but it's still there –there's no separation –it happens simultaneously with what's happening around us right now and then they slip right back out.

On Turtle Island some people especially white people are being programmed not to live in the spirit world. Somewhere in their psychc they have been programmed to be mass orientated, to control of the mind, which is the weakest control of all –the powerful control sits in the spirit. If someone with this mindset were in front of me now as I went into the spirit world I would loose him or her -but I know I can sit here and go quickly into that world without loosing you because of your spiritual orientation.

So I do relate to the story of these two simultaneously seeing the coyote because that coyote did exist. That part of native people does exist. I would not say it's lost because it exists on its own."

Shared belief in the spirit world was just one of several ties Black and Aboriginals found they had in common. Similar worldviews in regards to nature and ancestral spirits were also present. One of my particular areas of interest is in locating examples of what occurred with one another.

Chilean visual artist Andrea offers a perceptive insight into the investigation of possible syncretic beliefs. It is her view that altars are one of the best indicators of syncretic belief systems since altars contain representations of and offerings to important spiritual deities. Altars are thus important reflections of the spiritual cosmology of a people.

A look at altars in Brasil (named peij) that are used in the Umbanda religion and in African spiritualists churches in New Orleans (U.S.A) bear out this observation. The peijs in Brasil not only have representations of traditional African deities but also Aboriginal deities that are indigenous to the area. This bears witness to the fact that the Umbanda religion combines elements of both African and Aboriginal spirituality.

If one visits African Spiritualist Churches in New Orleans, not only will one find altars that will have offering to African saints but you will also find statues of Chief Black Hawk. Black hawk, who was a Sauk and Fox warrior who led a heroic resistance against the US government in the 1800´s. He is worshipped as a symbol of peace and justice in African Spiritualist churches. In Louisiana, his spirit, along with other

Aboriginal spirits like White Hawk are summoned in the course of worship to bring healing to those that need it.

During the course of my travels in Cuba, especially in the city of Santiago, I witnessed altars for the Santeria religion that had statues of Aboriginal figures, it was explained to me that they were for purposes of protection. Even though presently the exact origins of Aboriginal presence in Santeria ceremonies haven't been formally explored, an examination of Cuban history does provide some potential clues. Like numerous places in the Americas, there were joint slave and Aboriginal rebellions. Contrary to the popular mythology that the indigenous Arawaks were completely exterminated there are today still living in the Yatcras region of a few hundred miles from Santiago hundreds of descendants of Arawak Indians. Not only do they presently live separately in their own settlements but also there are Arawaks who live among the general Cuban population. Consequently, it is not farfetched to suggest that Arawak interaction with African people has resulted in syncretic beliefs.

There are other indicators other than altars that point to the possibility that African and Aboriginal interaction affect their respective spiritual practices. In Haitian voodoo practices Veve drawing of intricate designs in cornmeal is one aspect of voodoo that researchers haven't designated an African origin to. Anthropologist Maya Dereen felt that the designs were very similar to intricate Aztec and other Indians, who originally inhabited Haiti, were seafaring people who had contact with the Mayans and Aztecs.

Haitian voodoo group Boukman Esperyans had some perceptive observations on this connection. Band member Lolo in an interview with Errol Nazareth describes voodoo as not only an African religion but as an "Afro Indian religion" where the African spirit meets with the native spirit. Lolo also notes that the Haitian revolutionary Boukman united Africans and Natives to fight the French colonists in the 18 th century. He also makes the following comment "Africans and Indians see the world in the same way as we both see a parallel between the visible and the invisible world.

There are also other areas as yet to be fully explored areas of possible syncretic spiritual beliefs. One of these is the connection between the Muslim religion and the traditional Aboriginal belief.

Aboriginal Muslim researchers and activists such as Sr Maria Adin, Imman Benjamir Perez Mahomat and Br Mahir abdur Razzag are involved in investigating the spread of Islam among Aboriginal people over the last couple of centuries.

African Muslims explorers are believed to have traveled to North America centuries before Columbus; often they intermarried with Aboriginal people and never returned to Africa. This social interaction between Aboriginal and Muslims continued during the centuries of the trans Atlantic slave trade. As indicated in the July 1996 edition of the Muslim magazine "The Message", the fact that escaped African slaves joined the ranks of the Seminole Indians is not a secret. However, a previously undocumented fact was the existence and influence of African Muslim slaves who joined the Seminoles in the 1800´s with men wearing Muslin styled turbans and knee length or longer shirts. For ceremonial occasions the Seminoles wore ankle length turkey feather robes. Both the Cherokees and the Seminoles routinely covered their bodies in typically Muslin fashion.

What exactly occurred when Muslim and Aboriginal spiritual beliefs encountered each other raises some very key questions. I discussed this with John Beaubien, an aboriginal linguist of Mohawk ancestry who at one time used to attend Nation of Islam meetings. One of the immediate queries that he had was that he was be curious to know which Aboriginal traditional practices would be considered shirk (pagan) by African Muslims. For instance how would Muslims react to such things as the use of clan symbols or the belief in spirit helpers? Would these be considered shirk? We were both intrigued when we read and article by an aboriginal Muslim who was also a pipe carrier who attended sweats. Again we both had questions about how the two belief systems coexisted now and in the past. For instance the Cherokee women fought as warriors in many battles, what have been the reaction of African Muslims to this?

In addition to the Muslin/Cherokee/Seminole connection there is also the possible Muslin/Aboriginal/connection within the North American nomadic tribe of Ben Ishmael, a people who were a mix of African, white and Aboriginal people. Many of the families of the tribe of Ben Ishamel have Muslim names. This possible connection is also not limited to the North American continent. During the 16 th century, the governor of

Puerto Rico sent urgent communiqués to the Spanish government about the unrest that African slaves, specifically African Muslims, were creating on the island where they escaped and joined forces with the Aboriginal inhabitants.

Besides the obvious need for further scrutiny into Aboriginal and Muslim interaction, there are other areas that also warrant investigation. As evidence continues to accumulate indicating contact between African and Mayans and Olmecas, one wonders how culture's spiritual beliefs affected each other.

While it is important that we probe the past, there are contemporary links between various Black and Aboriginal spiritual beliefs I wish to examine.

An important and very sensitive area to explore is the increasing number of Black people who are utilizing Aboriginal traditional beliefs especially for the purposes of healing. I have reasoned with many Black people who have been aided by traditional Aboriginal spiritual practices such as the sweat. In an era when spirituality is viewed by many as another commodity to be purchased and where currently there are people like Lyn Andrews, who are willing to distort and manipulate spiritual practices to cater to these consumers; it is very important to present a viewpoint which adds an important dimension in terms of explaining the scenario.

Bob Manning is a Black psychotherapist, who among other things utilizes Aboriginal practices in his work counseling street kids, many of whom are Black. His success with using Aboriginal spiritual practices with Black youth is very revealing, especially in terms of the questions it brings up in regards to the Black psyche.

For the purpose of ensuring accuracy and complete context for this topic I am presenting a transcript of my conversation with Bob Manning.

B.M. I took some kids, some who were Black and who identified themselves as gay. Some white children, guys and girls who were involved in prostitution along with some gay white children and hooked them up with some macho Aboriginal kids. Then we took them down to La Pushe, dropped them off at this beach and told them they had to live together. It was a three-day retreat so we got tents and they backpacked down and I made sure they couldn't get out. It didn't work well at first. The straight kids were uptight at the gay kids and they hated each other and fought back and forth. Then one of the guys from the Indian center said we are going to do a talking circle. I wasn't sure how some of the kids were going to react. What happened that night was that the person who led the talking circle did a ceremony. He called it a council of people and what it is, was burning sage and cleaning yourself and getting rid of the negatives and bringing in the positives –each person cleansed himself. I expected some giggles from the kids that night but there wasn't and all of a sudden all this energy started focusing on this group that was on the beach at night time by this fire, under the moonlight –we went around to each person and smudged them and after that we all sat down and he said that he was going to pass an eagle feather to each person and they could talk about anything they wanted for as long as they wanted to talk. He didn't set any one about what to talk about –but everyone had to listen. No one could talk or interrupt, then the feather went from person to person after they were done –then they said all my relations and passed the eagle feather. When they said "all my relations" it meant that they were related to everything and everybody. Even though there was no theme that was stressed everyone talked about their pain and what was wrong with them and what they had gone through in their lives and each child heard that with other. They started becoming a community. They found that they had common pains, common issues and there were tears. It started when the sun went down and went on till almost the next morning and there were only forty people there. It was very powerful that night. I had been working all over the place: Chicago, New York, Los Angeles but I had never seen anything like this. We would take kids away for 3-day retreats and we would do the talking circle. More and more black kids were coming to these retreats and more Black children started feeling and sharing on a spiritual level what was happening in the talking circles. I was wondering why were Black children being pulled more into this. The feedback I was getting from the kids was that the talking circles were connecting them with the spirituality they felt they weren't receiving in religious institutions like the Baptist Church.

My feeling is that the Black man, the Black woman or Black children have not yet gone through the grieving process spirituality in the US and Canada.

D: Could you explain for people who might not know what the grieving process is?

B: Say for instance your mother was hit in a car accident – the first thing you might feel was shock –then you might feel anger and you have to work through that and people do that in different ways and with different processes. People can get stuck in the anger then there's fear, there's depression, there's more anger- if people can go through these levels of emotions and find a resolution then they can move onto the next stage, which is healing themselves and letting go. This is what I'm saying that Black people haven't been able to work through the processes, yet because the political and spiritual atmosphere of the US and Canada isn't giving them the chance to do that. I think the Baptist church, the Catholic church and Christianity has kept people from really going through the final part of the grieving process –we have gone through all these other things –that is why when something happens there are all these riots that take place, that's the anger part of the grieving process that hasn't yet come out –that is my feeling. If you look at the grieving process you realize that there hasn't been reconciliation. When Malcolm X started talking about this it freaked a lot of people out because the next step of grieving is to recognize and start talking about it -Malcolm was saying I have to drop my last name, because of slavery. He was recognizing the problem in order to the grieving. We have to resolve the grief. So a lot of us have turned to Aboriginal spirituality because it is the closest thing that we find helps us with these issues. The church might bring it out for us, however you are still reinserting a non-spiritual thing for something you want, which is spiritual so you will never get past a certain level. So I think sisters and brothers who are finding Native spirituality and discovering things through are really starting to break through the grieving process.

D: I was just having this interesting conversation with Ida Johns who is an Aboriginal of Coast Salish ancestry and one of the things we were talking about was I feel that on a psychic level, people of African descent living in North America are still trying to deal with that forced dislocation from Africa and that on a certain level we are in a state of disconnectedness from the earth here –this particular location we find ourselves in. This is not something that is really recognized and one of my observations is that it contains certain elements that begin to address the needs of Black people.

B.M. I agree with that –it's what I say is part of the grieving process and healing. Also, I think a lot of the symbols and elements are similar to what was used in Africa for healing purposes.

I think Black people are constantly looking for some element of spirituality. I really feel that the elements of Aboriginal people bring to us are very similar to elements that we need for our own healing process but it will never be the ultimate element that we need to find ourselves.

Interestingly, Aboriginal writer Jack Forbes in his book "Columbus and other Cannibals" had a parallel critique of Black Christianity. He feels that often-organized black sects lend themselves to dogmatism, narrowness and a concern with the petty and superficial. Black Christians would do well to look to their African Native origins instead of being dominated solely by the theology of their European oppressor. Thus this is what a lot of Black people have been intuitively doing!! Consequently, it is also not surprising the Rastafarian religion with its African orientation has also been very sympathetic to Aboriginal people as well as serving as inspiration to them.

Rastafarians like Mutaburaka have deep respect for Aboriginal spirituality. I was provided with a graphic illustration of this one night after reasoning with Mutaburaka on his midnight radio show "The Cutting Edge." During our discussion about Aboriginal people Mutaburaka spontaneously pulled out a book and read part of Chief Seattle's famous speech where he among things explains why the land is not for sale and the relationship between the creator and nature.

(Readers should know that in Jamaica "The Cutting Edge" is regarded by many including myself as the best "university" in Jamaica. Everyone especially young people in the ghettos stay up during the weekday night listen to the reasoning on the show).

The next day after my appearance on the show, I was walking down a road in a small country village. Stopping by a food stand for some fruit, I over heard a Rastafarian elder talking about last nights "Cutting Edge" show. He remarked that the thing that moved him the most was to hear the speech by the "Indian Chief". To my amazement, he had written part of it down and began reciting it. This person had no idea that I was the guest on the show and this incident has stuck in my mind as an illustration of how aboriginal and Rastafarian spiritual sentiments can be in sync with one another.

Dub poet Oku Onuru said the following to me while we were talking about our experiences at Aboriginal ceremonies.

"I heard their singing and chanting and it reminded me of being at a nyabingi (A Rastafarian spiritual gathering.) They are like Rasta – they are earth people. They are like us they sit and watch –they know what you do it will come back to you. So when they look at New York they think like we do that it's heading for destruction because that's the natural order of the earth."

Vancouver, Berkeley 1990

Vancouver, Berkeley 1990

With four hours to kill before my bus to Berkeley I decided to stop in at the Vancouver Public Library. While there I selected a number of books on colonial Mexican history and carried them to one of the tables. A friend had mailed me a letter written to a hip-hop magazine from Mexico where a fan made reference to Afro-mestizo culture in that country. Now I was trying to dig deeper to find the roots of this Blakk Indian history. It seems that when that country had a sizable Black population, there were so many Africans marrying Aboriginal people that the governor actually tried to outlaw Blakk Indian marriages. Undoubtedly, the successful Blakk Indian-led revolts in Mexico, which created autonomous maroon settlements like the quilombos in Brasil, had something to do with this reasoning. The successful maroon settlements established by the Blakk Indian rebel leader Yanga in Veracruz is just one example. Later on in its history the Mexican government gave sanctuary to Blakk Indian warriors from the Seminole Nation, during their war with the United States. The revolutionary fighter Zapata himself was of Blakk Indian heritage and Mexico had a Blakk Indian president, Vincent Geurrero.

As I poured through the books I was interrupted by an old black man sitting across from me. He had a stack of books on ancient Egyptian history in front of him. In a deep bass voice with an American accent he started speaking to me about ancient Egypt. He had some very perceptive things to say so I sat and listened attentively as he spoke about the religious and scientific practices of the ancient Egyptians.

After about twenty minutes he stopped speaking and asked me what I was reading about. I explained what I was investigating. He looked at me and smiled.

"First thing is you should be looking more closely at Egypt. That connection is stronger there than most people realize. What you are studying is my history too. My father's side of the family is pure Indian! I am going to explain something important to you. When I was a child my grandmother explained to me certain histories of what used to happen on the Plains with the Indians. You ever hear when black kids are playing and they say 'Buffalo Gal on the outside on the outside?'" I replied that I remembered hearing an old rap song that had that phrase. "Well back in the old days when the cavalry would go out traveling they realized that the Indians would hesitate to kill Black women. So what the white soldiers would do is they would travel with Black women on the outside of them like a shield because they realized that most times the Indians would not attack them if the black women were the one's exposed. They would hide behind the black women or buffalo gals as they were called back then. That's the true meaning of what is behind that children's rhyme, "Buffalo gal on the outside on the outside."

His explanation made me recall another history that had been told to me by an Aboriginal woman from Mexico, Martiza Hurtzail. She was now living in Toronto where she had a son named Tecumseh with a Blakk Indian man, Dimitri Corrmel. His great grandfather had been a runaway African slave who had been given refuge and adopted by the Choctaw people in Alabama. He died defending Choctaw territory against attacks by the US. Cavalry. He repelled two attacks killing seven soldiers in the process before a fresh squad of soldiers murdered him. Still his efforts allowed his Choctaw wife and their children to escape.

* * *

I broke up the long bus journey to Berkeley with a short stop in Washington State. There I hooked up with Pablo B an aboriginal filmmaker, traditional dancer and a hip hop industrial musician. Music labels especially aboriginal companies rejected his work because they found it strange that an aboriginal kid would be composing industrial music mixed with hip-hop.

That night Pablo and a Black anarchist friend jammed in his living room. I watched as they created a new track with Pablo rapping as the anarchist quickly scribbled lines for him a piece that railed against the FBI campaigns against Black and Aboriginal Activists like Geronimo Pratt, Leonard Peltier and Anna Mae Aquash. Over raw jagged hip-hop beats Pablo rapped lines that were very pertinent at the time.

"State police power increasing every hour, black men shot with their hands held high."

The high number of fatal shootings of unarmed black men in Canada and the United States weighed very heavily on people's minds.

Frequently during my travels in North America I would encounter aboriginal youth who were hip hop fans and rappers who were also heavily influenced by black political figures like the Black Panthers and Malcolm X. Aboriginal rappers like Julian B and his CD "Once Upon A Genocide" and Funkdoobius were just few of the aboriginal rappers emerging at this time. At a Toronto Pow Wow I was blown away by the knowledge of an aboriginal hip-hop designer named Cyril Sunbird who was conversant in radical Black politics. As we spoke he revealed to me that his aboriginal father had grown up in the american deep south. Not having a chapter of the American Indian Movement in his area his father joined the local Black Panther chapter.

What can occur when hip-hop radical black politics and conscious aboriginal youth converge was further illustrated by what I witnessed one night on a downtown Toronto street corner.

A group of aboriginal youth was hanging out after a concert. Among them was 'Hip Hop Mohawk.' We had met after an aboriginal sovereignty meeting. While I was leaving the meeting, I noticed that the person walking beside me was wearing a baseball cap with a beaded Public Enemy insignia on it. I inquired where he got his cap. He responded that he had beaded it himself because he was a long-standing fan of the rap group and hip-hop in general. 'Hip Hop Mohawk' (who was indeed from the Mohawk nation) was also well versed in the spiritual practices of Black and Aboriginal people.

One of the other aboriginal youth present that night was my friend, Sid Bobb. He had been buying Public Enemy records from a very young age. In fact I used to pass on Public Enemy paraphernalia that P.E.'s Chuck D had autographed for Sid. Both of Sid's parents had been heavily involved in radical aboriginal politics. His mom Lee Maracle used to work with the Black Panthers when they would travel to Vancouver.

That night after the concert another aboriginal youth whose uncle was a cop, started attacking rappers who were against the police. Sid answered him back with one of the most articulate defenses of rappers with anti-police stances that I have ever heard. Sid had no delusions about the police and their role in propping up the status quo regardless of their colour. He understood that often when rappers attacked the police they were also exposing deeper issues of racism and injustice. Everyone stood quietly in awe as Sid dropped science about this, quoting Malcolm X and the Black Panthers in the process.

I spoke with Bob Manning a black counselor who does extensive work with aboriginal and black street kids. He provided me with his insights into the affinity aboriginal youth have for hip-hop. According to him "there is a great need for aboriginal youth to have that arrogance that black people have on television. Just recently I was in the Squamish nation in British Columbia, I saw a lot of Malcom X shirts and a lot of flap jackets. These were aboriginal kids imitating black kids in ghetto communities that they see out of Detroit television. Aboriginal kids are going through the same things black kids are. A search for identity, the anger, the need to make something that's theirs

–whether its their own name, their own gang its that need to reach out for the extended family, just like black kids try and do. Some end up in gangs, which become their extended family. Aboriginal youth tend to look to black people as a model because black people are the first to come out with that arrogance. It was the same thing in the sixties –when the Black panthers came out other groups like the American Indian Movement started following the Panthers. Some black people are very quick at saying, "Hey we don't like this and we are going to change it and if you don't like the changes –fuck you! It's this arrogance that got black people out of slavery and which stimulated numerous slaves revolts. It's the attitude of people refusing to be controlled. The need and want to be free. So when an Aboriginal kid in Squamish sees a black kid in Detroit being arrogant, wearing a flap jacket and saying "Hey, this is me and I'm going to get in your face, I've had enough of this, I am going to fight right here, I'm going to take a stance." Aboriginal kids relate to that and more and more are adapting that stance as we witnessed at the standoff at Oka."

When I arrived in San Francisco there was intense political activity as people geared up to protest the Gulf War that was about to erupt. I stopped off at the anarchist book store Bound Together Books to meet with anarchist hardcore band M.D.C. in regards to a Blakk Indian project. I left with the brilliant book, Black Wheels of Anger about radical activist, Tom Mooney by the anarchist writer Peter Plate who distributed his books free of charge in the tradition of the Diggers: anonymous radical activist of the sixties who use to hand out free goods to people in San Francisco's Golden Gate Park.

I met with Michael Franti who was also preparing to take part in a Gulf War protest. Speaking with Michael was one of the key reasons I had journeyed to Berkeley. We had become acquainted while he was still with his first band, the Beatnigs. Now he was getting ready to launch his new band Disposable Heroes of Hiphoprisy. Michael had just recently discovered the fact that he was of Blakk Indian heritage. He introduced me to two Blakk Indian women Amelie Prescott and Akiba Tiamaya. Both had fascinating life stories to speak about.

Amelie began by telling me "When I was growing up I was told I was Creole but my parents never spoke what that mixture really was. As a child some people asked me if I was Black. I lived in Maryland in the fifties and there was still a lot of segregation going on but I never took it personally. It was just kind of interesting to me when I got sent to the back of the bus. So my Mom made me wear a little Aboriginal bracelet at the beginning of the summer so I could show I had a tan so I didn't have to go to the back of the bus or have to go to the coloured bathroom. In the early sixties I was living in San Francisco and teaching a mixed classroom in Sausilitio. I taught a pilot program in Black studies and sex education. For my Black studies course I felt it would be good to have some of the black Panthers I knew come over and talk about the subject. I spoke to them and they agreed. Twice a week they came and taught Black studies. Now, they used to ask me to decide what race I was because there was going to be a revolution and I would have to take sides. They would say 'Are you Black or White?' and I would say 'I'm brown, I'm aboriginal, I'm black, I'm French, I'm a mixture.' That was my first introduction talking about that because those things weren't discussed. Aboriginal people weren't in fashion then."

Her encounters with the Black Panthers prompted Amelie to further investigate her Blakk Indian heritage. She began to teach in East Oakland and discovered that a lot of her students were part aboriginal. As she taught about aboriginal ways, parents of students would approach her and say that someone back in their family was aboriginal but it wasn't something that was spoken about.

Wondering about this silence prompted Amelie to do some research. What she discovered was the history of escaped slaves going to aboriginal reservations where they would be together and have babies. Then the army could come and say, 'Everybody out.'

Everyone would go. Blakk Indians had no tribal rights so they couldn't say, 'I'm half Choctaw. I'm half this.' Those tribal rights were gone and that is what the army and government wanted."

Amelie stated that during those times "it was very dangerous to be an aboriginal person so if you could pass for Black you didn't mention you were part aboriginal since you could get killed because of that or have your children taken away to missionary schools.

They would often take the children away and put them in white homes. A lot of children who are mixed Black and

Aboriginal don't know. People like Michael Franti who was adopted, didn't know until I told him and he went and found his birth mother and she told him he was."

Amelie's friend Akiba Tiamaya had some further observations about this according to her. Amelia said aboriginal people were considered nothing so a lot of time they would be in the Black community and hide out there. They were considered black. "A lot of black people today haven't seen the necessity to come forth. Its like, so what? My grandmother was aboriginal, so what? It wasn't any big deal"

Akiba herself had experienced some difficulties as she tried to reconnect with the aboriginal side of her heritage. At various times she hadn't felt welcomed in aboriginal communities. A very spiritual person, she was proud of the fact she was a sun dancer but even in that she had to overcome obstacles from aboriginal people. In conversation with me Akiba disclosed something that I have heard echoed by many Blakk Indian people. She said that she had experienced a lot of inner turmoil because in this time when it seemed to her so many people were falsely attaching themselves to aboriginal culture, she didn't want to be perceived as being part of that bandwagon.

She was also acutely sensitive to the possibility that aboriginal people might think that she was claiming this part of her ancestry in order to have access to certain economic rights aboriginal people have. Like so many Blakk Indian people I have spoken to, Akiba felt aboriginal people had been so mercilessly exploited that in no way did she want to participate in anything that could possibly further exploit them.

As a result many Blakk Indian people are very quiet about the aboriginal side of their heritage.

After speaking with Amelie and Akiba, Michael and I went to San Francisco where intense preparations were taking place for a massive demonstration against the US. Bombing of Iraq. Accustomed to and aware of the practice of police brutality and the reality of class warfare at demonstrations some activists were practicing their tactics to deal with the police.

Later that night as Michael and I took part in a gigantic march, we discussed what Amelie and Akiba had spoken to me. As Michael put it to me, "I have tended to identify mostly with being Black because that is predominantly what other people's perception of me is. But I've always had a sense of a fact that I'm Native American. Being both Native American and African American I feel as though part of me was stolen from my country and I had my country stolen from me."

The keynote speaker at the march was Angela Davis renown Black activist and professor at the university of Berkeley. Angela gave a rousing speech. I would later find out that she was very aware of the Blakk Indian connection.

According to her, "It's really important for us as Black people to stand together with our American Indian sisters and brothers because they really helped us during slavery. A lot of our ancestors were able to escape and set up maroon communities that were created by fugitive slaves that were the result of the work our Native sister and brothers did for us and of course a lot of us have Native blood. I don't think it makes any sense to talk about it if you aren't going to do something about it. We have to say that the genocide that was perpetuated against the original inhabitants of this land came around to Africans. We were all together then and we ought to be together today."

Bridget Walker: One of the many Blakk Indians in America

Tribute to Black Panther Party Founder Huey Newton

Montreal and Kahnawake

Montreal and Kahnawake

It was with great anticipation that I arrived at the International Feminist Book Fair. The gathering was noteworthy for the large number of published aboriginal women authors present. Writers like Jeannette Armstrong, Chyrstos, Lee Maracle, Beth Brant and Joy Harjo were at the fair. The gathering later took on added significance as it marked the occasion where aboriginal women confronted white feminists like Anne Cameron on their racism, privilege and their appropriation of aboriginal stories. In the midst of all this debate everything was interrupted by an emergency presentation by a Mohawk women, Donna Goodleaf. She spoke passionately to the gathering about a political crisis and hostilities being directed against her people by the province of Quebec and the Canadian government. After her presentation a number of Black women came up to her to lend their support. At the forefront of this group were Kate Rushin and Audre Loudre.

Kate Rushin had written the brilliant title poem for an anthology of radical women of colour entitled a "Bridge Called My Back". A few years earlier I had been traveling through the USA and passing through Boston I had called her up and asked to speak to her about her writings. At that point I had run out of money and I was very hungry. I was really touched when she arrived at our meeting and she pulled out sandwiches and fruit she had brought for me so I could have something to eat. Her act of compassion for a total stranger was something I never forgot.

I had a wonderful conversation about Blakk Indian history with Audre Loudre who in person exuded great warmth and friendliness. Her writings had always been a source of great inspiration to me especially her book, "Sister Outsider" with essays like "Your silence Will Not Protect You" was one of my all time favorite books for the manner in which it encouraged people to be courageous in their daily lives.

Speaking with Donna Goodleaf I found that she was just as conversant with radical black politics as she was with radical aboriginal politics. Years later I would meet up with her again where she was teaching a course on indigenous politics at an aboriginal educational institute. One of the textbooks she made her aboriginal students study was the autobiography of Assata Shakur. The account of this Black Panther (herself of Blakk Indian ancestry) who was targeted by the US government and who after their attempts to kill her managed to escape from a maximum security jail and escape to Cuba where she now lives in exile.

From the Feminist Book fair I decided to hitchhike to Kahnawake where a Pow Wow was being held.

I managed to arrive at the Kahnawake Pow Wow just in time for Grand Entry. (This was when all dancers taking part in the Pow wow made their entrance).

Pow Wows were gatherings I really looked forward to. It was an opportunity to reconnect up with old friends and swap stories.

While getting some corn soup I noticed this black guy enter the Pow wow grounds. Something about his facial features reminded me of other Blakk Indians I had encountered in the American southern states. I approached him and introduced myself. His name was Brian Teach and it turned out I was right. He was part Choctaw with a deep interest in researching black Indian history. A while back he had been traveling up in northern British Columbia and up in the Yukon area. He found out African sailors had been in that region and ended up intermarrying with the Inuit who lived there. Brain said a few years later he was in Montreal and he spied what he thought was an African American woman walking down the street. He greeted her and later while conversing with her found out to his great surprise that she was from up north and was a mixture of African and Inuit. I told him about my wonderful experiences traveling in Greenland where so much of the Inuit population were reggae fans to the point where the Inuit Minister of Culture confided that she listened to Bob Marley records everyday.

Later on I spotted my friend Neil who is Cree from James Bay. A professional photographer, he was taking pictures of the Pow Wow for a new aboriginal magazine. He pointed out to me a young aboriginal girl who was practicing her dancing off to the side. She was wearing a beautifully designed red, green and gold Bob Marley t-shirt! It was quite a sight to see the combination of beadwork, feathers and Bob Marley's visage. I was reminded of the time when I was at a Pow Wow on Odawa territory watching this fancy dancer doing traditional dance steps in full regalia. All of a sudden out of nowhere he started incorporating hip hop, break dancing and moon walking moves into his routine and then with a big smile on his face quickly resumed his traditional fancy dancing!! (A quick chat with him revealed that he was a break-dancer when he wasn't fancy dancing!).

An aboriginal deejay that liked to play techno, jungle and dub told me the story of being at a Pow Wow and hearing a drum group incorporate a refrain from a popular rap song in a drum song. While standing up beside a drum group who were rehearsing, a traditional singer called Andy, himself a big reggae fan approached me, pointed to my dreadlocks and out of the blue, just said "You know that the famous Cree resistance leader Poundmaker who fought with Metis leader Louis Riel had dreadlocks down to his ankles". He gave the name of a photography book that I could find a picture of Poundmaker.

Sure enough when I later purchased the book I found that there was a picture of Poundmaker and he had really long dreadlocks, which he apparently refused to cut. This photograph would later turn out to be an inspiration for a reggae track entitled "Poundmaker's Dub" which would feature aboriginal traditional singing mixed with dub music.

One night while surfing the net I came across a website for an association of Black Native Americans. The site had amazing pictures of Blakk Indians at recent Pow Wows including pictures of Black Navajo women.

New Orleans

New Orleans

It was a hot and muggy late night in New Orleans. I was trying to locate the Glass House, a bar that was renown for its black Indian musical particles. After having to stop and ask for directions many times I finally made it to the famous bar. To my great disappointment I found that it was closed. The bar had been my best bet for locating members of New Orleans famous Mardi Gras Indians.

Having just gotten off a long train ride from New Mexico I wasn't about to just give up. I decided to just keep walking and see if I could find another musical practice.

My journey there had been inspiring by a breathtaking book of photography called, "Spirit World", by New Orleans photographer Michael P. Smith. The author spoke of Black and Blakk Indian groups (tribes) whom dressed/masked as aboriginal people.

According to Smith,

"Each year tribe members create and hand sew their own costumes, often ordering off at great expense for exotic beads and plumes. Spare time throughout the year is devoted to these masterpieces of dress arts. Individuals spend huge sums of money on their vestments. Each Mardi Gras Indian costume is elaborated constructed with variations of paper mache, eggshells, broken glass, seashells, ribbons, rhinestones, ostrich, peacock and turkey feathers, plumes, glass beads, sequins, velvet sparkle all organized into a fantastic explosion of funk and flash, with head-dresses, staffs, pipes, hatchets, skulls and other embellishments –all intended to humble the viewer with their power, spirit and beauty."

It was his belief that the design, sewing and beadwork were some of the finest examples of Afro American art. I wanted to talk directly with the people in this art form so I kept walking down the streets and alleyways. The further I walked the more run down the neighborhood became and besides passing the occasional sports bar where people were watching Monday night American football, the streets were pretty much deserted. After walking for a good 90 minutes I stopped to rest in front of the bar where people were spilling out into the street during an intermission in the football game.

Just then, one of those unbelievable coincidences that occasionally occur when one is on the road happened! As I was picking up my bags to continue walking two of the men coming from the bar asked me if I had any cigarettes. I replied I didn't but there was something incredibly familiar about the face of one of those men. For the life of me though I couldn't put my finger on what the connection was. I started conversing with them. I explained how I had come to New Orleans inspired by Michael Smith's photography book. At that point the man whose face seemed familiar stopped me and said "I know Michael Smith, in fact there is a picture of me in that book sewing and preparing my outfit". Then it all clicked into place as I remembered seeing his picture in "Spirit World".

He introduced himself as Bubble and his friend Randy. Bubble was a member of the "Wild Magnolias" one of the best know Blakk Indian tribes who had an album of their recording released internationally. They invited me to walk to their home a couple blocks away to continue our conversation. As we walked they cautioned me against walking alone in this neighborhood so late at night. When we reached Randy's house we sat on the veranda steps outside since it was so hot and muggy.

Randy and Bubble took the time to give me an insight into behind the scenes preparation for the highlights of the Blakk Indian calendar the parade on St. Joseph day. On this day the streets are full of Blakk Indian dressed resplendently in outfits modeled on aboriginal regalia. Some have traced these Blakk Indian parades to as far back as 1870's.

Bubble explained to me how in the months preceding St Joseph day he would spend up to 14 hours day sewing and preparing his outfit often going without sleep in the days preceding the parade as he worked around the clock to make certain his outfit was just right. The completed outfits were intricate pieces of art where the premium was on originality and creativity. Bubble told me how some outfits could weigh up to a hundred and fifty pounds. Participants would then march twenty to thirty miles wearing these heavy outfits. As Bubble was providing me with the details out of the corner of my eye I noticed this car cruising at a caterpillar pace along the street. Eventually it went past us. I wasn't the only one who had noticed it. Randy nudged me and whispered "did you see that the guy in the passenger seat had a shotgun in his hands trained out the car window?"

Without skipping a beat we continued our conversation; I asked Randy and bubble given the obvious aboriginal influence in the outfits, if the parade in some manner was attempting to honor the original aboriginal inhabitants of the state. Part of my motivation for asking this question was what I had observed in carnivals and other parades in other parts of the world. In Jamaica, the Bahamas, Haiti, Trinidad and the Labor Day parade in New York I have witnessed Black and Blakk Indian people dressed in outfits modeled after aboriginal regalia. With traditions like John Canoe in Jamaica and Bahamas where you find participants at this festive events dressed as the original aboriginal inhabitants of the islands, the Arawak Indians. John Canoe parades started out of a tradition created by African slaves. Implicit in these parades from my viewpoint is an attempt by Africans to pay homage to and show respect to the aboriginal inhabitants of the islands.

Randy and Bubble felt that there were several elements in the Black Indian parades and other aspects of Black culture in Louisiana that paid homage to the aboriginal people who first inhabited this land. Louisiana's history contains accounts of Seminole, Natchez and Choctaw Indians joining African slaves in uprisings against plantation owners. Some of the most famous Blakk Indian participants are in fact both Black and aboriginal ancestry. A Blakk Indian spiritual and cultural link is something that has always been a constant presence. As one of New Orleans most famous Blakk Indian musical alumni the Neville Brothers sing in the movie "Posse",

that's my blood down there
on the reservation
All the Indian nations
that's my blood down there
on Mother Africa
All the first Americans
its my blood down there.

In New Orleans one can go to African Spiritualist churches where aboriginal spirits like those of Sauk and Fox Chief Black Hawk occupy a revered position in places of worship. In the Black Indian musical practices where participants meet to practice and ready themselves for St Joseph day there are constant references in music and verse to aboriginal people. Bubble felt that honoring the aboriginal spirits and presences was are in fact of essential aspect of the black Indian parades. As photographer Michael Smith states,

"When Blacks dressed as American Indians they were assuming the composite identity of a spiritual people who fought and died for their way of life and belief. Masking Indian was and is a rite or ritual for spiritual guidance."

Black Indian masking

Halifax

Halifax

Fog was everywhere on the morning that I pulled into the coastal community of Halifax, the capital of Nova Scotia. My time in Halifax was going to be very brief yet I knew this was a location rich in black history. My first stop was the main public library.

My experiences have been that often librarians are not only some of the most knowledgeable sources of information about local history but often when you least expect it they can also be very politically subversive. The elderly seemingly conservative librarian in Halifax certainly didn't disappointment me in this regard; ordering on my recommendation cassettes about the Black Panthers and radical aboriginal movements for the library in addition to giving me a perspective on black history in Nova Scotia.

Numerous black families in Nova Scotia exhibit great pride in the fact their families have roots in the community that go back hundreds of years. Canadian history books hold up the European Samuel de Champlain as the great explorer in Canada's north coast. Matthew Decoste was Champlain's interpreter when he traveled down the St Lawrence River and along the northeast coast of Canada. Decoste was an African and he was Champlain's Micmac/French interpreter.

Speaking with me, historian Afua Cooper raised certain questions about history books' treatment of Decoste. She wondered why books state that he was Portuguese African and left it at that. She brought up the issue of how did Decoste come to learn Micmac? Afua`s point is that he must have been there before to learn the language and become an interpreter.

According to oral tradition Mathew Decoste married a Micmac woman and their descendants are still around. (It is not difficult to find Blakk Indian families in Nova Scotia who have Micmac ancestry). In regards to the point of Decoste being described as Portuguese African, it falls into the whole pattern of what was transpiring on the northeast coast. Back then Portuguese fishing boats came every year to Labrador and Newfoundland to take fish back to Portugal. Even if Decoste was a slave at the time Portugal had a lot of Blacks living there by way of the Muslim Moorish Empire.

I wandered into the Native Friendship Center in Halifax, Nova Scotia. Some youth were just hanging out waiting for a drum practice to begin. Others were just sitting and reading. I recognized the man in front of me quietly reading. His name was Donald Marshall. A racist Canadian justice system had railroaded this Micmac Indian into prison where he had spent many years in jail for a crime he didn't commit. Now he had finally been released. Years later his protest to the courts arguing the fact that Micmac Indians had the rights to fish year round would result in the ruling by the Supreme Court called the Marshall decision. The courts recognition of Micmac fishing rights would spark heated confrontations and a further reminder of the continuing battle for recognition of aboriginal rights in Canada.

It was also in Halifax that during the late sixties a Black Nova Scotia activist Rocky Jones generated massive public attention to the issue of racism in the province when he arranged for Black Panthers from the United States to come to Halifax. A generation later racism was still a burning issue in Canada. Both black and aboriginal people were angry and pressing for their rights. A hip-hop track comes on the campus radio station its entitled, "Aboriginal Hitch Hike Rap". Black and aboriginal protests are its theme. The lead rapper it turns out is the son of Rocky Jones.

Windsor, Detroit

Windsor, Detroit

The Canadian town of Windsor is now separated by a 10-minute bus ride for the American city of Detroit. A few centuries before, this same route was a key point in the Underground Railroad that used to smuggle fugitive slaves into Canada from the United States. Aboriginal people in the region frequently gave aid to black runaways who made it across the border. The Tuscaorara are just one example of aboriginal people who provided assistance to Black runaways. Thus it is possible to find Blakk Indian families in this region who can trace their ancestral roots to this time period.

My interest in Windsor had began a couple of years before when a friend had given me a copy of an album by a Blakk Indian jazz musician Mixashawn who used to play with the highly regarded jazz outfit Ronald Shannon Jackson and the Decoding Society. Mixashawn who plays tenor sax had a musical group with his brother Rick Rozie called Afro-Algonquin. The group created jazz music that sought to showcase their particular mix of aboriginal music with Black musical forms. When I spoke with him Mixashawn had just finished playing at a memorial concert for the great aboriginal jazz musician Jim Pepper. Like another Blakk Indian musician Jack Dehonnette (whose 1993 CD "Fifth World" explores Blakk Indian jazz roots) Mixashawn is a musician who feels that musical forms like blues, gospel, and rock n roll have many connections to traditional aboriginal music. Rock n roll guitar legend Jimmy Hendrix, who himself was of Blakk Indian ancestry and who wrote songs like "Don't live today" about aboriginal people; informed journalist that tracks like "Little Wings" had an obvious aboriginal influence.

Communicating with Mixashawn via telephone resulted in my learning one of the many history lessons that one is unable to find in textbooks.

Mixashawn is from the Mohegan people who refused to live on reservations. They maintained property in the Windsor area north of Hartford until the1930s when due to the Depression they lost their land and dispersed into other areas such as Hartford. When the Aboriginal community in Windsor broke up many were blakk Indians, so they went into the ghettos and remain there today. As a result many Blacks and Latin people have aboriginal blood and some have vigorously maintained traditional Aboriginal ways. Mixashawn stated that he had met blakk Indians in the ghettos who still have pipes and drums from their grandfathers.

At the time our conversation in the early nineties the Mohegans were seeking access to land in near Hartford to perform traditional aboriginal ceremonies. Due to the fact that they refused to define themselves by colonial boundaries and complicated no doubt by the fact that many are Blakk Indians who don't look stereotypically aboriginal; the Mohegans were encountering many obstacles in their quest to have access to the land.

All of this was in my mind as I crossed the border from Windsor into Detroit to meet with a member of the Detroit techno Underground Resistance (UR). The group is known for its anonymous and radical political stance coupled with its groundbreaking music. Many of Underground Resistance records contain coded political message whether inside the musical tracks or inscribed on strategic places on the vinyl itself. One can find many coded referenced to aboriginal people and aboriginal resistance leaders, especially in releases on their Red Planet label. UR had recently played a very successful gig in Toronto to support the Lubicon Cree and their longstanding fight against logging companies.

The member of UR that I met with (whose name is not disclosed in keeping with the anonymous policy of the group) explained to me that he was of Blakk Indian ancestry. When he informed me that his sister was a pipe carrier well versed in traditional aboriginal spiritual practices, the words of Mixashawn ran through my head. Modern Blakk Indians exist in places in North America that the general population wouldn't associate with an aboriginal history.

Musician Mixashawn

Black Indian Resistance

Black Indian Resistance

For the outnumbered European colonialists, one of their biggest fears was of an alliance between African slaves and aboriginal peoples. They had concrete examples of what could happen when this alliance occurred.

Mexico experienced its first widespread wave of slave insurrections in the period 1560-80. The Spanish colonialists had increased the number of African slaves brought into the country to work in mines and estates. By the 1560s, fugitive slaves from the northern mines were terrorizing regions from Guadalajara to Zacateca, allying with the Indians and raiding ranches. Viceroy Martin Enrique noted that in 1572 and 1574 that "cooperation between Negroes and Indians made repression all the more difficult and requested aid from Spain."

The fear of Black and Aboriginal as people is not something that is dated, it continues on today in contemporary life and politics.

One of the most intriguing and certainly different spins on this fear comes from Canadian communications theorist Marshall McLuhan. In a Playboy interview during the 1960s, he stated, "the cultural aggression of white America against Negroes and Indians is not based on skin colour and belief in racial superiority, whatever ideological clothing may be used to rationalize it but on the white man's inchoate awareness that the Negro and Indian as men with deep roots in resonating tribal world are actually physically and socially superior to the fragmented and alienated and dissociated man of western civilization. Such a recognition, which stabs at the heart of the white man's entire social value system inevitably, generates violence and genocide. It has been the sad fate of the Negro and the Indian to be tribal men in a fragmented culture, men born ahead of their time."

While I feel that his opinions come from a very romanticized view of Black and aboriginal people and I certainly don't agree with his casual dismissal of white supremacy, I do find it somewhat noteworthy that an essentially non-political but renown white scholar in his own manner is acknowledging and attempting to analyze white people's fear of Black and Aboriginal people.

I met with aboriginal author and historian Jack Forbes, who has conducted extensive research on this subject. He pointed out to me that about twenty years ago an article was published in the Journal of Negro History entitled "Divide and Rule." It detailed what was called "The South Carolina Policy." This was the colonial policy in South Carolina that was developed specifically to make First Nations afraid of Africans and vice versa. According to Forbes, this policy was somewhat successful in that the different African rebellions were separate from the First Nations rebellions without the two forces helping each other. By playing one group against the other, even though they were a small minority, the whites managed to survive through this successful "divide and rule" policy.

This fear of a Black and Aboriginal alliance has also, in my opinion, manifested itself in the attempted erasure of the joint history of African and aboriginal people. Both Jack Forbes and author Doug Sivad point to the following glaring omission in terms of recent document American history as one example of this.

In the summer of 1526, Spanish colonialist Lucas Vasquez de Ally landed at the mouth of the Peedee River in present day South Carolina with a hundred Spaniards and one hundred African slaves from Haiti. Malaria, raids by aboriginal people and ultimately a slave revolt forced the Spanish colonialists to flee after a short period of time. The African maroons who remained established a settlement and prospered, friendly to some aboriginal people, foes to others. Since no African women were brought during early African slavery, these Africans intermarried with Aboriginal people. This Blakk Indian settlement predates any of the other European settlements recorded in the history books, yet it is difficult to find acknowledgment of this fact.

Jack Forbes feels one of the causes for this is what he calls the "White Hub" of scholarship. Academic research has privileged Europeans, making them the centre of activity. Everyone that the Europeans have contact with is on the periphery. Consequently, scholars will examine the relationship between White people and Black people or the relationship between white people and Aboriginal people but rarely will they examine the relationship between Black people and aboriginal people.

This kind of thinking has also permeated the minds of the general western population. In North America, I have always been puzzled by most of the discussions I've heard on the subject of "interracial marriage." Most people using this term refer to the union of a white person with another person of colour. For some reason, people discount the possibility that an interracial marriage may also refer to the union of people of colour from different racial backgrounds -Chinese and Black, for instance.

The repercussions of this kind of thinking can be easily seen by an examination of cinema. "Daughters of the Dust" by Julie Dash was the first film that I have seen which depicted a union between an African and an aboriginal person. As Julie Dash said in an interview with bell hooks, "There are certain tribes that were absorbed within the black community to the point where you couldn't distinguish Native American features. They just look African American. And to my knowledge that intermarrying has never been depicted on the screen, a Native American and an African American mating, bonding creating a life together that wasn't just built upon some lust of the moment. I wanted to show that."

There are other political ramifications that arise from the denial and attempted erasure of joint African and Aboriginal history. One of these centers around the issue of land. As Jack Forbes said to me, "White society doesn't want African Americans putting forward claims and saying yes we are part Native people, you owe us something not just for slavery, but you owe us something else because we are native people, we were here first, we have a claim to this land."

Land has always been one of the primary tools that the United States government has used to cause separation and friction between Black and aboriginal people. When I was in New Orleans, photographer and historian, Michael P. Smith explained to me the "Red Bone" communities were prevalent in Louisiana. These communities were created when aboriginal people went to sign treaties with the government. The government would tell them we can't give you land since you aren't really "Indian" — there are too many Black people among you. So the aboriginal people would return and create communities on the outskirts of their communities where they would send those among them that looked "too black." Afterwards they would return to the government and say we are only Aboriginal people living here, we deserve land.

Jack Forbes also pointed out the case of the Freedman people in Oklahoma. They were citizens of various tribes in Oklahoma, who were also of African ancestry. In the 1890s, when the tribes were broken up by a government act, those who the government considered Aboriginal people by blood were given land in individual parcels that were protected by a trust status. As a consequence of their looking "too African," the Freedmen were given their land without trust protection, which generally meant that their land went on the market and whites were able to get a hold of it. By contrast, those aboriginal people who received their land with trust protection had sale of their land restricted, which continues today.

Due to the fact that they looked "too African," the Freedmen weren't even allowed to record even their degree of aboriginal blood, even though they were citizens of the Cree and Cherokee nations. As a result, they had no continuing legal relationship with the US government as aboriginal people. These ties were completely severed. A situation that Jack Forbes feels is a violation of treaties, a violation of law, and a potential area of litigation. Maneuvers like these by the US government were very common. When one considers for example that on the east coast of the U.S., practically every tribe is a mixture of African and First Nations one begins to understand the potential scope of litigation that could be brought by Blakk Indian people against the US government.

(Coincidentally, after I wrote this paragraph I picked up a newspaper and read that aboriginal people had put forward a claim to Ellis Island in New York. To me, this is just the tip of the iceberg of the potential land claims that could be brought against the US government).

There are some contemporary examples of the empathy Black people feel for Aboriginal people in North America. It may be this empathy that past and present settler governments have feared. Later on, I will critically examine the reality of political alliances between Black and Aboriginal people. First I would like to present some of the contemporary real life stories that have been passed on to me and which are not found in history books.

I remember sitting in the kitchen of the Vancouver home of Lee and Dennis Maracle when Lee, a prolific writer and First Nations activist shared these stories with me.

"We saw the empathy of Black people for Indians during the Longest Walk

(An aboriginal political march across the US). A friend of ours had to leave her car in the city — so she said I will leave it in a Black ghetto so if it gets stolen at least Black people will get it. So she parked this car, which had the "Longest Walk" bumper sticker in this ghetto and left it. Six months later, she went back to the neighbourhood and to her surprise the car was there as she left it; and all the Black people who greeted her in the neighbourhood told her that they had looked after the car for her.

Dennis had experiences of going to this school during the 1960s where there were a lot of Black and White confrontations. One day they were having a riot at the school where the Black kids were beating on these white kids in the corridor and Dennis came walking through. It was like the parting of the Red Sea — the Black kids let him walk through the fighting totally untouched because they could see that he was Indian.

One day while sitting on the lawn of the Native Friendship Centre in Toronto, I spied a friend of my brother, a Black musician named Kerwin. We started chatting away and the following conversation ensued.

"You can ask your brother from way back, I always said, you know, I'll give my sympathy to the Native people first before I give it to Black people because it's their land. My father would always show us books and films like newsreels of Malcolm X and the ones that depicted how the Indians were massacred and the buffalo slaughtered. Let me tell you something that happened in high school. It was 1973; the teacher's name was Mr. Fagen. He was our history teacher and he was always Sir Winston this and Sir Winston that, so I got up and said, why don't you tell the whole truth, what the settlers did to get this land, how they stole, how they killed the Indians.

"Well, you know how White people can get really red — well, this guy turned totally red and he pointed to me and said, "You sit down!" When I sat down, he pointed to me again, his face still red and said, "You get up and get out of here. Go to the principal's office." So, I went to the principal's office where they suspended me for a week. They called my father, who was really proud of me and really angry with them. He told them, "You just want to suspend him for telling the truth."

A sampling of contemporary African American rap and poetry reveals a lyrical rendering of this empathy.

Take a piece of America back
but who had if first hear the Indian Curse
Public Enemy

How we gonna make the Black Nation rise?
Remember the so-called Indian, look what
they did to him — maybe they'll do that to us!
Brother D.

The blues have been ripped off like jazz,
ripped off like the Indians, ripped off like the land
Gil Scott Heron

The Fire This Time issued their single "Oka Ain't Over" drawing the parallels between the government assault on Aboriginal people and the numerous police shootings of innocent Black people.

Whether it has been acts like raising the Aborigine flag during their Australian tours or addressing chapters of the American Indian movement, rap group Public Enemy has always been ready to support indigenous movements worldwide. Unknown to the general public is the behind scenes communications that Chuck D from Public Enemy has had with Aboriginal youth and the warriors who were involved at the standoff at Kahnesatake.

While a guest on the Canadian literary television show "Imprint," Harry Allen, Public Enemy's "media assassin" threw a lot of the listening public totally off guard when he accepted a welcome from the host Daniel Richler by stating, "thanks for having me on your stolen land." Later on the show, he caused further consternation when addressing the issue of white racism he raised concerns of both Black and aboriginal people. While this confounded those who expected him to be "pro-black" and only address "Black" concerns, his comments were enthusiastically greeted by Aboriginal and Blakk Indian people watching the show. In fact, his comments formed the foundation for The Fire This Time track "Basslines and Ballistics."

Dub poet Binta Breeze, on a Canadian tour, continued to speak out about the injustice facing aboriginal people in Canada despite the torrent of criticism she received from raising the issue.

One of the most moving and profound demonstrations of support for First Nations people that I have witnessed occurred at a Fugees, Ben Harper and Spearhead concert at the Opera House in Toronto in 1993. This was a year when rap was under violent attack by the media who were intent on categorizing it as violent and sexist. After a moving performance by Ben Harper (who is another artist of Blakk Indian ancestry) and the Innocent Criminals, headliners Spearhead took to the stage. Earlier that evening I had given Spearhead founder Michael Franti a copy of the book of aboriginal philosophy, The Native Creative Process, by Jeannette Armstrong and Douglas Cardinal.

Franti and another member of the band began their show by stating that they first had to show respect for the aboriginal people's whose land they were on. Myself and many in the audience were both surprised and touched when he then read a passage of Native philosophy to the hushed capacity audience, who responded with huge applause. The group then performed their piece "Of Course You Can," which contains the refrain, "One day the indigenous people of this earth are going to reclaim the land that is rightfully theirs."

As a footnote, a few years later, I was walking in downtown Toronto and ended up in conversation with some young Aboriginal street kids. One of them was listening to some music on his Walkman. I asked him what he was listening to. "Spearhead," he replied. "I was at a concert a while back and this group came out and paid respect to my people and I have been listening to them ever since."

(I wish to make it clear that by no means do I consider the aforementioned stories to be the full sum of acts by musicians and poets in support of Aboriginal people. There are many, many more. However, these just happen to be the ones that I've been privy to and wish to share).

Travelling through North America in the late 1980s, I had the opportunity to meet with two women, one African American, the other aboriginal. Both had been influenced by political and spiritual thought from each other's culture to the point that they had transformed their lives and dedicated it to these principles.

I had been hitchhiking in Arizona and New Mexico with my destination being the Navajo Nation Fair in New Mexico where my friend John Williams and his all-aboriginal reggae band "Native Roots" were going to be playing. I had arrived at the Navajo Nation Fair in a torrential thunderstorm. Sloshing through the mud trying to find the concert site, I noticed this white van that was parked on the fair ground. It was covered with a beautiful painting of Bob Marley, Malcolm X, Peter Tosh and Marcus Garvey. As well, in huge red, gold, and green lettering it also said "Stop Police Violence" and "How Can You Call the Cops on Cops!"

Soon I was talking with the owner of the van, a Navajo woman named Cimi Boone. She was selling medicinal herbs and T-shirts that had a picture of Bob Marley on it with the caption "How Can You Call the Cops on the Cops." Not surprisingly, the police had hassled her entering the fairground with her van.

Cimi had been inspired by the words of Bob Marley, Peter Tosh, Malcolm X, Marcus Garvey and Martin Luther King. She now identified herself as a Rastafarian as she felt there were so many things within the Rastafarian beliefs, which were in tune with her First Nations beliefs.

Following the example of Black radicals, she had devoted her life to fighting the system and trying to live outside of it as much as possible. She had helped organize a group, which fought against police violence.

This group was a coalition of Aboriginal, Black, Latino and white people who had been harassed and brutalized by the police. Part of their campaign was to draw attention to the fact there was no mechanism to address the wrong doing of the police — hence the T-shirt with the caption "How Can You Call the Cops on the Cops."

Now she was living in her van travelling to different First Nations communities with information about people like Marcus Garvey and Bob Marley as well as literature about the campaign against police brutality.

She had given birth to her son at home and had purposely not registered him at the hospital or with the social security system. She had done this because she didn't want the "Babylonian" system to have any knowledge of his existence. This would further facilitate his remaining outside of the system.

In Vancouver, Canada, my friend Farah Shroff introduced me to Dale Edwards. An African American now living in Vancouver, she dedicates her life to activism in support of Aboriginal people. She had been particularly inspired by the political philosophy of George Manuel, an aboriginal political figure from the Shuswap nation. George Manuel's philosophy of being self-sufficient also led her to change specific areas in the way she lived her life. From Aboriginal people in Mount Currie she learnt various skills on how to live off the land so she could be less dependent on needing money from the system to survive.

I spoke to George Manuel in 1985. Even though he was ill and confined to a wheel chair at the time, he was still a fiery and inspiring orator. He was still feared by the Canadian settler government, as indicated by the RCMP officers that I observed monitoring him. Throughout his life, Manuel had drawn the ire of the Canadian settler government. Not only did he work and strategize towards a unified Aboriginal political force in Canada, but also he was especially visionary in the manner in which he strategized and examined the situation of indigenous peoples all over the world. It was George Manuel who coined the phrase "fourth world" to refer to the collective state of indigenous people around the world. He traveled extensively throughout South and Central America visiting indigenous communities as well as to Africa where he met with and was inspired by the policies of Tanzanian's then-president Julius Nyerere. While he worked in the Canadian city of Ottawa, he frequently met with African diplomats who were also working there. George explained to me the strategies and experiences of African peoples in their fight against colonialism was something that had been very important to him. This influence can be seen in an excerpt from an address he made to an aboriginal political organization. “The African subjugated people cry out for UHURU (freedom),” he wrote. “The Indian people should cry out both for UHURU and unity for it is only through unity that we will have real freedom.”

While there exists many more acts of Black and Aboriginal political solidarity, I feel at the same time it is essential not to romanticize the reality of this alliance. It’s also necessary to try and clearly put into perspective the significance and potential benefits of this alliance. A successful alliance requires a solid foundation built on mutual respect and understanding of the similarities and differences in perspectives and agendas of the groups involved. Various forces such as colonialism, miseducation, different historical and spiritual experiences and practices have prevented black and aboriginal people from completely understanding each other’s political perspectives and agendas. It has also been difficult to access accurate accounts of each other’s histories and philosophies.

Many Black and Aboriginal people have understood the need to address this by owning and controlling their own educational and information resources. From my perspective, understanding the links between Black and Aboriginal struggles is of utmost importance. However, so is the need to always keep in mind the larger political picture within which all struggles occur. The importance of this approach becomes apparent as one observes black and aboriginal people who decide to support the destructive forces of capitalism and state power. All over the world, among situations of great poverty, there is always Aboriginal or Black elite who plays their part in the process of exploitation. Critical analysis of state structures and state power is vital. Anarchist thought and practices (which has numerous precedents within black and aboriginal cultures) has made a valuable contribution in this regard.

Books like "African Anarchism the History of a Movement" by Sam Mbah and I. E Igariwey (See Sharp Press 1997) provide important details about these anarchist traditions.

One of the values of Black and Aboriginal peoples having a better understanding of each others cultures and histories is the potential strengthening and enrichment that can occur from them having contact with one another.

Black psychotherapist Bob Manning is an example of how this can occur. After being exposed to traditional aboriginal healing practices, he was able to incorporate this knowledge into his healing methods and consequently provide more effective counseling for street kids.

Some Black and Aboriginal people have drawn upon their respective historical experiences and philosophies to come up with radical political analysis. When these various analyses are combined, they have the ability to improve the tools that can be used for radical analysis. The benefits of a combined Black and Aboriginal political analysis obviously have the potential to benefit more than just Black and Aboriginal people. The possibilities of how this can occur is vividly illustrated by an essay "The Need For Alternatives in understanding The Struggle of the Lubicon Lake Cree", by Sumita Bidaye, a writer of South Asian decent. In this essay, she is able to overcome the shortcomings of radical eco philosophies in being able to analyse the situation facing the Lubicon Lake Cree. She does this by utilising the philosophy and political analysis of Black activist and MOVE founder John Africa combined with analysis provided by the American Indian Movement. From her viewpoint, radical eco philosophies are unable to adequately address the role of colonialism in the case of the Lubicon Lake Cree. By drawing on the analysis provided by Black and Aboriginal people who have been directly affected by colonial domination and genocide, she is able to provide more that the usual conclusion of "environmental injustice" that is arrived at by environmentalists.

This is just one example of how Blakk Indian political philosophies can advance political struggle.

ABOUT THE AUTHOR

Searching for the knowledge that has been left out of the pages of history books has been a long standing passion for me. Finding that has meant not being satisfied with just going to libraries and scouring academic tomes. To locate that knowledge I have committed myself to endless hours on buses, trudging alone on dusty roads, climbing mountains in remote locations and surviving near perilous encounters with military forces. It has meant trusting and relying on the goodwill and information of strangers and the wisdom that our elders have to offer us. It has meant listening and observing quietly waiting patiently for the tiny scrap of information that could possibly open up a new world of information. Sometimes these arrive in unexpected forms like when I was approached by a Native American hip-hop fan who explained that his father had joined the Black Panther party in the American south because there were no Native American political organizations operating there at the time. Other times it has simply meant trusting my instincts as in the time when in the Bolivian mountains I had seconds to decide whether to jump in the back of a truck heading to an unknown location, (I decided to and the result was an incredible experience in a Blakk Indian coca growing community). Music, art, spirituality, resistance politics are vital to me and hence figure predominantly in all my observations in this book.

Made in the USA
Coppell, TX
22 March 2025

47385980R00114